Human Rights

Editor: Danielle Lobban

Volume 442

First published by Independence Educational Publishers

The Studio, High Green

Great Shelford

Cambridge CB22 5EG

England

© Independence 2024

Copyright

This book is sold subject to the condition that it shall not,
by way of trade or otherwise, be lent, resold, hired out or otherwise
circulated in any form of binding or cover other than that in which it
is published without the publisher's prior consent.

Photocopy licence

The material in this book is protected by copyright. However, the
purchaser is free to make multiple copies of particular articles for instructional
purposes for immediate use within the purchasing institution.
Making copies of the entire book is not permitted.

ISBN-13: 978 1 86168 902 3

Printed in Great Britain

Zenith Print Group

Acknowledgements

The publisher is grateful for permission to reproduce the material in this book. While every care has been taken to trace and acknowledge copyright, the publisher tenders its apology for any accidental infringement or where copyright has proved untraceable. The publisher would be pleased to come to a suitable arrangement in any such case with the rightful owner.

The material reproduced in **issues** books is provided as an educational resource only. The views, opinions and information contained within reprinted material in **issues** books do not necessarily represent those of Independence Educational Publishers and its employees.

Images

Cover image courtesy of iStock. All other images courtesy of Freepik, Pexels, Pixabay, and Unsplash.

Additional acknowledgements

With thanks to the Independence team: Janey Jills, Klaudia Sommer and Jackie Staines.

Danielle Lobban

Cambridge, May 2024

Contents

Chapter 1: What Are Human Rights?

Understanding human rights	1
Everything you need to know about human rights	2
Human Rights Act	4
What is the Universal Declaration of Human Rights?	7
Human rights: a legacy of the Holocaust	10
5 ways the European Convention on Human Rights makes the UK a better place	12

Chapter 2: Human Rights Today

From Gaza to Ukraine, what would the pioneers of human rights think of our world today?	14
People's rights are threatened everywhere, from wars to silence about abuses, rights group says	16
The universality of human rights needs defending	17
The long shadow of Qatar's human rights abuses	19
Qatar World Cup workers suffered 'human rights abuses', new Amnesty report finds	21
World Cup: FIFA must press for binding human rights commitments from 2030 and 2034 hosts	24
What is modern slavery?	26
Modern slavery is increasing – 1 in every 150 people are victims	28
Modern slavery in the United Kingdom	30
Ten ways that Saudi Arabia violates human rights	34
The silent chains of Saudi Arabia: my fight for my daughter and our freedom	35
12 women activists and leaders making the world a better place	37
Young activists share their vision for human rights	40

Useful Websites	42
Glossary	43
Index	44

Introduction

Human Rights is volume 442 in the **issues** series. The aim of the series is to offer current, diverse information about important issues in our world, from a UK perspective.

About *Human Rights*

Human rights are basic standards necessary for a life of dignity, equality, and respect. However, sometimes human rights are undermined or ignored. In this book, we look at the history of human rights, human rights law, and human rights issues.

Our sources

Titles in the **issues** series are designed to function as educational resource books, providing a balanced overview of a specific subject.

The information in our books is comprised of facts, articles and opinions from many different sources, including:

- Newspaper reports and opinion pieces
- Website factsheets
- Magazine and journal articles
- Statistics and surveys
- Government reports
- Literature from special interest groups.

A note on critical evaluation

Because the information reprinted here is from a number of different sources, readers should bear in mind the origin of the text and whether the source is likely to have a particular bias when presenting information (or when conducting their research). It is hoped that, as you read about the many aspects of the issues explored in this book, you will critically evaluate the information presented.

It is important that you decide whether you are being presented with facts or opinions. Does the writer give a biased or unbiased report? If an opinion is being expressed, do you agree with the writer? Is there potential bias to the 'facts' or statistics behind an article?

Activities

Throughout this book, you will find a selection of assignments and activities designed to help you engage with the articles you have been reading and to explore your own opinions. Some tasks will take longer than others and there is a mixture of design, writing and research-based activities that you can complete alone or in a group.

Further research

At the end of each article we have listed its source and a website that you can visit if you would like to conduct your own research. Please remember to critically evaluate any sources that you consult and consider whether the information you are viewing is accurate and unbiased.

Issues Online

The **issues** series of books is complemented by our online resource, issuesonline.co.uk

On the Issues Online website you will find a wealth of information, covering over 70 topics, to support the PSHE and RSE curriculum.

Why Issues Online?

Researching a topic? Issues Online is the best place to start for...

Librarians

Issues Online is an essential tool for librarians: feel confident you are signposting safe, reliable, user-friendly online resources to students and teaching staff alike. We provide multi-user concurrent access, so no waiting around for another student to finish with a resource. Issues Online also provides FREE downloadable posters for your shelf/wall/table displays.

Teachers

Issues Online is an ideal resource for lesson planning, inspiring lively debate in class and setting lessons and homework tasks.

Our accessible, engaging content helps deepen students' knowledge, promotes critical thinking and develops independent learning skills.

Issues Online saves precious preparation time. We wade through the wealth of material on the internet to filter the best quality, most relevant and up-to-date information you need to start exploring a topic.

Our carefully selected, balanced content presents an overview and insight into each topic from a variety of sources and viewpoints.

Students

Issues Online is designed to support your studies in a broad range of topics, particularly social issues relevant to young people today.

There are thousands of articles, statistics and infographs instantly available to help you with research and assignments.

With 24/7 access using the powerful Algolia search system, you can find relevant information quickly, easily and safely anytime from your laptop, tablet or smartphone, in class or at home.

Visit issuesonline.co.uk to find out more!

Chapter 1: What Are Human Rights?

Understanding human rights

Human rights are an important part of our lives. They help ensure that every person, regardless of who they are or where they come from, is treated fairly and with dignity. In this article, we will explore what human rights are, why they matter, and how they can make a positive impact on our world. So, put on your explorer's hat and let's dive into the fascinating world of human rights!

Human rights – what are they?

Human rights are the basic rights and freedoms that every person is entitled to. They are universal, which means they apply to everyone, no matter where they live or what they believe. These rights are protected by the law and are meant to ensure that all individuals are treated with respect and fairness.

There are many different types of human rights, covering a wide range of areas such as:

1. **The right to life:** This means that every person has the right to live and be protected from harm.
2. **The right to education:** Every child has the right to go to school and learn.
3. **The right to be free from discrimination:** Nobody should be treated unfairly because of their race, gender, religion, or any other reason.
4. **The right to be heard:** Every person has the right to express their opinions and be listened to.
5. **The right to be safe:** People should be protected from violence, abuse, and exploitation.

Why do human rights matter?

Human rights are important because they help create a fair and just society. They ensure that everyone has access to the same opportunities and can live a life free from discrimination and harm. By respecting and protecting human rights, we can build a world where everyone is treated equally and with dignity.

One of the key principles of human rights is that they are interdependent and indivisible. This means that all human rights are important, and they cannot be separated or traded off against each other. Think of human rights as pieces of a puzzle that fit together to form a complete picture of a just and inclusive society.

Human rights in action

Human rights are not just abstract ideas – they are put into action every day to make a difference in people's lives. Governments, organisations, and individuals work together to uphold human rights and ensure that they are respected and protected.

Sometimes, human rights issues can be complex and require creative solutions. For example, let's say there is a child who wants to go to school but cannot because they live in a remote area without access to transportation. In this case, human rights activists may work to provide transportation or establish a school closer to the child's home, ensuring their right to education is fulfilled.

It's important to remember that promoting human rights is not just the responsibility of governments and organisations. Every one of us can play a role in making a difference. We can start by treating others with kindness and respect, standing up against discrimination, and speaking out when we see someone's rights being violated.

Exploring human rights further

If you're interested in learning more about human rights, there are many resources available to help you explore further. Issues Online, for example, offers a wide range of interactive resources that provide comprehensive and up-to-date information on human rights. These resources can be accessed anytime and anywhere, allowing you to continue your learning journey no matter where you are.

In addition to online resources, you can also engage in discussions with your friends, family, and teachers about human rights. Ask questions, share your thoughts, and listen to different perspectives. This will help you develop a deeper understanding of this important topic and encourage critical thinking.

Human rights are the building blocks of a fair and just society. They ensure that every person is treated with dignity and respect, regardless of their background or beliefs. By understanding and respecting human rights, we can make a positive impact in our communities and create a better world for everyone. So, let's continue our exploration of human rights and work towards a brighter future together!

Everything you need to know about human rights

Human rights are the basic protections that everyone has. But where do they come from? Join us on a journey through key human rights developments in history and find out how we are protected today.

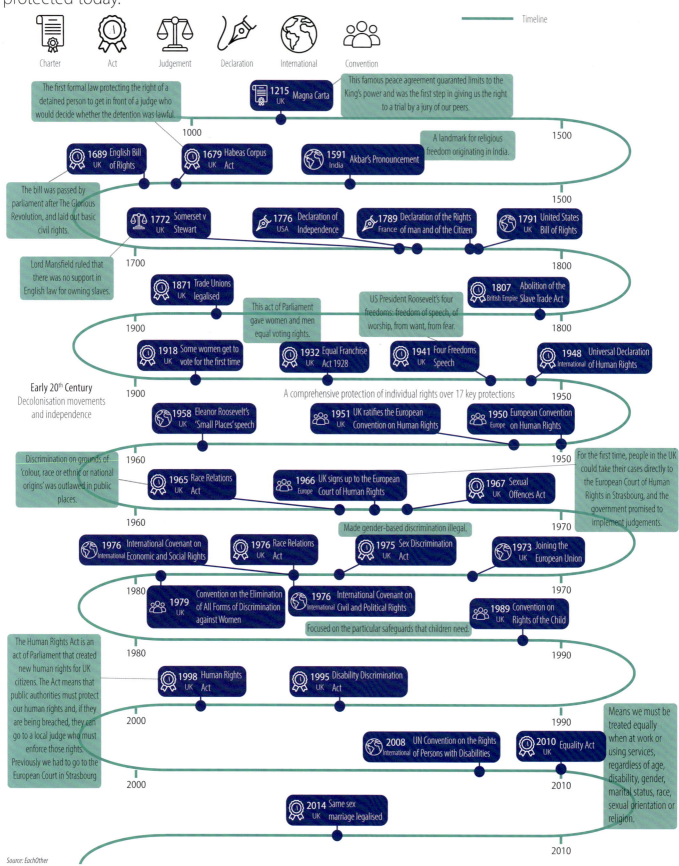

Source: EachOther

issues: Human Rights — Chapter 1: What Are Human Rights?

The three main ways your rights are protected as a UK citizen

1 Public authorities, including government, must not act in a way that breaches your human rights. And nobody should discriminate.

2 If you find your human rights are being breached, then you can take the case to a judge in the UK which must enforce them.

3 If that doesn't work, as a last resort you can take your case to the European Court of Human rights in Strasbourg.

Our rights today
You have these key enforceable rights from the European Convention

1 The state's obligation to respect human rights

2 Right to life

3 Right not to be tortured

4 Right not to be enslaved

5 Right not to be unlawfully detained

6 Right to a fair trial

7 No punishment without law

8 Right to family and private life

9 Right to freedom of thought, conscience and religion

10 Right to free expression

11 Right to free association

12 Right to marry

13 Right to an effective remedy if your rights are breached

14 Right not to be discriminated against

Protocol 1   Article 2 Right to education

Protocol 1   Article 1 Right to peaceful enjoyment of property

Protocol 1   Article 3 Right to fair and free elections

Source: EachOther

The above information is reprinted with kind permission from EachOther.
© 2024 EachOther.

www.eachother.org.uk

issues: Human Rights   3   Chapter 1: What Are Human Rights?

Human Rights Act

Find out about the UK's Human Rights Act (1998). Learn more about what the Human Rights Act is, who it applies to, who it protects, and what it aims to do.

What are human rights?

Human rights are fundamental rights and freedoms that we are all entitled to as human beings, irrespective of our nationality, race, gender, gender identity, religion, sexual orientation, citizenship, or other status. Human rights are universal – they belong to everyone – and are not granted to people by the state.

Human rights are protected in international law. There are many international treaties and agreements that ensure that states around the world respect and protect people's human rights, and many states have their own domestic laws to protect human rights at home.

Our human rights mean we are free to live as we choose, without abuse, mistreatment, or interference from the government and other public bodies. They protect equal access to fundamental services and institutions like healthcare, education, democratic elections, and fair judicial processes.

What is the Human Rights Act?

The Human Rights Act (1998) gives us legal protection of our basic human rights in the UK. The legislation ensures that the rights set out in the European Convention on Human Rights (ECHR) are enjoyed by us all, which includes things like dignity, fairness, equality, tolerance, and respect.

What is ECHR?

The ECHR, also known as the European Convention on Human Rights, is an international human rights treaty between the member states of the Council of Europe. Britain played a central role in designing the ECHR in the aftermath of the Second World War, aimed to protect human rights, democracy, and the rule of law.

The Council of Europe – which isn't the same as the European Union – is Europe's leading human rights organisation, and is made up of 46 member states, including the UK.

How many human rights are there?

There are 16 human rights outlined in the Human Rights Act (1998). Each right is referred to as a separate article:

- Right to life (Article 2)
- Right not to be tortured or treated in an inhuman or degrading way (Article 3)
- Right to be free from slavery and forced labour (Article 4)
- Right to liberty and security (Article 5)
- Right to a fair trial (Article 6)
- Right not to be punished for something which wasn't against the law when you did it (Article 7)
- Right to respect for your private and family life, home and correspondence (Article 8)
- Right to freedom of thought, belief and religion (Article 9)
- Right to freedom of expression (Article 10)
- Right to freedom of assembly and association (Article 11)
- Right to marry and start a family (Article 12)
- Right not to be discriminated against in relation to any of the rights and freedoms listed here (Article 14)
- Right to peaceful enjoyment of possessions (Protocol 1, Article 1)
- Right to education (Protocol 1, Article 2)
- Right to free elections (Protocol 1, Article 3)
- Abolition of the death penalty (Protocol 13, Article 1)

What does it look like when human rights aren't respected and protected?

The Holocaust is an infamous example of human rights abuses on a massive scale (also known as a crime against humanity). This gave rise to the 1948 Universal Declaration of Human Rights, which recognised and guaranteed 'dignity and worth of the human person.'

Today, in the UK, we can see clear examples of the erosion of the rights and freedoms of refugees and asylum seekers, which signals the gradual weakening of the freedoms and protections afforded to all people in the UK.

Can human rights be taken away?

Human rights cannot be taken away, however in the UK most human rights are qualified or limited. This means that most rights can be restricted under certain circumstances as outlined in the Human Rights Act.

In a democratic society, respecting and protecting the human rights of everyone is a balancing act. For example, the right to freedom of expression of someone who is inciting racial hatred may be restricted to protect other people's rights not to be subjected to abuse or harassment based on their race.

Qualified rights

These rights can be restricted by a public authority if it is in the interest of the wider community, or to protect the rights of other people. These rights may only be interfered

with under certain circumstances as specified by the Human Rights Act.

If a public authority interferes with a qualified right, the Human Rights Act says that it must show that it has a lawful, 'legitimate aim' for doing so.

These are examples of legitimate aims:

- The protection of other people's rights
- National security
- Public safety
- The prevention of crime
- The protection of health.

Limited rights

These rights come with some exceptions but only as specifically outlined in the Human Rights Act.

For example a person's Right to liberty may be limited if a person is convicted of a crime and is sentenced to serve time in prison.

Absolute rights

Some rights set out in the Human Rights Act are absolute. By law these rights should never be interfered with for any reason, not even during war or public emergencies.

One of the absolute human rights is Article 3: the right to freedom from torture and inhuman and degrading treatment.

Which legislation protects human rights?

The Human Rights Act (1998) is the main legislation that protects your human rights in the UK. The protections defend rights like your right to life, a fair trial, and freedom of expression.

However, the Human Rights Act is not the only instrument that protects human rights in the UK. Our human rights and freedoms are also protected in other domestic laws and by other international human rights treaties, which have been signed and ratified by the UK. This means that the UK has agreed to be legally bound by the laws of these treaties.

When did the Human Rights Act come into effect?

The Human Rights Act passed through both parliamentary Houses, later gaining royal assent in November 1998. The act came into force in October 2000.

Who does the Human Rights Act apply to?

The Human Rights Act applies to all public authorities in the UK. A public authority is an organisation that provides public services or performs public functions. Examples of these include: central and local government; police; immigration services; courts; schools; prisons; and NHS hospitals or social services.

Private organisations or charities that perform public services or functions are also considered public authorities, and must follow the law of the Human Rights Act. An example of a situation where a private organisation is considered a public authority is a private hospital funded by, and providing care on behalf of, the NHS.

The Human Rights Act sets out the principles for how public authorities must treat all people in the UK. The ultimate aim is that all people are treated with dignity, respect, equality and fairness.

'The Human Rights Act protects the rights of all people living in the UK. There are no exceptions.'

Who does the Human Rights Act protect?

The Human Rights Act protects the rights of all people living in the UK. There are no exceptions.

A person's race, age, nationality, citizenship, gender, gender identity, sexual orientation, or any other status, do not matter when it comes to human rights and protection under the Human Rights Act in the UK.

Asylum seekers and refugees are also protected under the Human Rights Act.

Why was the Human Rights Act introduced?

The Human Rights Act was introduced to enshrine the human rights outlined in the European Convention on Human Rights in domestic UK law, allowing a person to take legal action through the UK's justice system if their human rights are violated by a public authority.

After the atrocities of the Second World War, the ECHR was drafted by the Council of Europe – the UK is a founding member of the Council, and British lawyers played a key role in drafting the convention – to protect the human rights and freedoms of the people of Europe.

The Human Rights Act draws on the ECHR, bringing protection for human rights into UK domestic law. This means that if a person's human rights have been breached they can take their case to a UK court, rather than having to apply to the European Court of Human Rights in Strasbourg, France, to seek justice.

What does the Human Rights Act aim to do?

The Human Rights Act ensures that public authorities, such as central and local government, respect and protect the human rights of all people living in the UK by making the protection of human rights a matter of domestic law. If public authorities violate a person's rights the matter can be taken to a UK court.

The principles and values of equality, fairness, dignity, and respect are also expressed, promoted, and upheld through the Human Rights Act.

Asylum seekers, refugees and the Human Rights Act

Asylum seekers and refugees are also protected under the Human Rights Act. Asylum seekers, refugees and stateless peoples are particularly vulnerable to human rights abuses.

Importantly, the Act is clear in stating that: *'No one shall be subjected to torture or inhuman or degrading treatment or punishment.'*

Asylum seekers, refugees, and Article 3 of the Human Rights Act

Article 3 of the Human Rights Act is key in protecting asylum seekers and refugees from being returned to countries where they face the risk of torture, harm, or death.

However, proving that someone is at risk of persecution in their country of origin can be difficult. In the case of someone seeking asylum in the UK, they can provide evidence of their persecution at their asylum interview, and in some cases, evidence of torture.

This right also protects asylum seekers and refugees (along with anyone else) from torture and inhuman and degrading treatment while they are in the UK.

In 2012 a case was brought against the Home Secretary for delaying welfare support to two asylum seekers who became homeless and destitute while awaiting a decision on their fresh asylum claims.

The court ruled that in this case the Home Office's policy on delaying welfare support for asylum seekers had caused homelessness and destitution. The policy of delaying consideration for support was also declared unlawful, as it risked violating Article 3 of the Human Rights Act.

How we campaign to protect human rights

At Freedom from Torture we stand with survivors to protect their rights here in the UK and abroad.

We work alongside survivors to raise awareness and campaign for torture survivors' rights in the UK, on key issues such as detention, decision-making, and poverty. We also stand together to hold torturing states to account.

12 February 2024

Design

Design a poster displaying the 16 human rights

The above information is reprinted with kind permission from Freedom from Torture.
© 2024 Freedom from Torture

www.freedomfromtorture.org

issues: Human Rights

Chapter 1: What Are Human Rights?

What is the Universal Declaration of Human Rights?

When was the UDHR created?

The UDHR emerged from the ashes of war and the horrors of the Holocaust. The traumatic events of the Second World War brought home that human rights are not always universally respected. The extermination of almost 17 million people during the Holocaust, including six million Jews, horrified the entire world. After the war, governments worldwide made a concerted effort to foster international peace and prevent conflict. This resulted in the establishment of the United Nations in June 1945.

On 10 December 1948, the General Assembly of the United Nations announced the Universal Declaration of Human Rights (UDHR) – 30 rights and freedoms that belong to all of us. Seven decades on and the rights they included continue to form the basis for all international human rights law.

Who created the UDHR?

In 1948, representatives from the 50 member states of the United Nations came together, with Eleanor Roosevelt (First Lady of the United States 1933-1945) chairing the Human Rights Commission, to devise a list of all the human rights that everybody across the world should enjoy. Her famous 1958 speech captures why human rights are for every one of us, in all parts of our daily lives:

'Where, after all, do universal human rights begin? In small places, close to home – so close and so small that they cannot be seen on any maps of the world. Yet they are the world of the individual person; the neighbourhood he lives in; the school or college he attends; the factory, farm, or office where he works. Such are the places where every man, woman, and child seeks equal justice, equal opportunity, equal dignity without discrimination. Unless these rights have meaning there, they have little meaning anywhere. Without concerted citizen action to uphold them close to home, we shall look in vain for progress in the larger world.'

Hansa Mehta was the delegate of India, and the only other female delegate to the Commission. She is credited with changing the phrase 'All men are born free and equal' to 'All human beings are born free and equal' in the Declaration.

Various delegations contributed to the writing of the Declaration, ensuring the UDHR promised human rights for all, without distinction. The Egyptian delegate confirmed the universality principle, while women delegates from India, Brazil, and the Dominican Republic disrupted the proceedings to ensure the gender equality. Other delegations disrupted the attempts by the Belgium, France, and UK delegations to weaken provisions against racial discrimination.

> 'That's why we celebrate the UDHR, not because of who wrote it into history, but because of those who used it to disrupt history.' – Agnes Callamard's keynote address to Amnesty International's 2023 Global Assembly

Why is the UDHR important?

The UDHR marked an important shift by daring to say that all human beings are free and equal, regardless of colour, creed, or religion. For the first time, a global agreement put human beings, not power politics, at the heart of its agenda. Communities, movements, and nations across the world took the UDHR disruptive power to drive forward liberation struggles and demands for equality.

Although it is not legally binding, the protection of the rights and freedoms set out in the Declaration has been incorporated into many national constitutions and domestic legal frameworks. All states have a duty, regardless of their political, economic, and cultural systems, to promote and protect all human rights for everyone without discrimination.

Our human rights in the UK

The UDHR has three principles: universality, indivisibility and interdependency.

1. **Universal:** This means it applies to all people, in all countries around the world. There can be no distinction of any kind: including race, colour, sex, sexual orientation or gender identity, language, religion, political or any other opinion, national or social origin, of birth or any other situation.
2. **Indivisible:** This means that taking away one right has a negative impact on all the other rights.
3. **Interdependent:** This means that all of the 30 articles in the Declaration are equally important. Nobody can decide that some are more important than others.

A summary of the 30 articles of the Universal Declaration of Human Rights

The 30 rights and freedoms set out in the UDHR include the right to asylum, the right to freedom from torture, the right to free speech, and the right to education. It includes civil and political rights, like the right to life, liberty, free speech, and privacy. It also includes economic, social and cultural rights, like the right to social security, health, and education.

What are the UDHR articles?

- **Article 1:** We are all born free. We all have our own thoughts and ideas and we should all be treated the same way.
- **Article 2:** The rights in the UDHR belong to everyone, no matter who we are, where we're from, or whatever we believe.
- **Article 3:** We all have the right to life, and to live in freedom and safety.
- **Article 4:** No one should be held as a slave, and no one has the right to treat anyone else as their slave.
- **Article 5:** No one has the right to inflict torture, or to subject anyone else to cruel or inhuman treatment.
- **Article 6:** We should all have the same level of legal protection whoever we are, and wherever in the world we are.
- **Article 7:** The law is the same for everyone, and must treat us all equally.
- **Article 8:** We should all have the right to legal support if we are treated unfairly.
- **Article 9:** Nobody should be arrested, put in prison, or sent away from our country unless there is good reason to do so.
- **Article 10:** Everyone accused of a crime has the right to a fair and public trial, and those that try us should be independent and not influenced by others.
- **Article 11:** Everyone accused of a crime has the right to be considered innocent until they have fairly been proven to be guilty.
- **Article 12:** Nobody has the right to enter our home, open our mail, or intrude on our families without good reason. We also have the right to be protected if someone tries to unfairly damage our reputation.
- **Article 13:** We all have the right to move freely within our country, and to visit and leave other countries when we wish.
- **Article 14:** If we are at risk of harm we have the right to go to another country to seek protection.
- **Article 15:** We all have the right to be a citizen of a country and nobody should prevent us, without good reason, from being a citizen of another country if we wish.
- **Article 16:** We should have the right to marry and have a family as soon as we're legally old enough. Our ethnicity, nationality, and religion should not stop us from being able to do this. Men and women have the same rights when they are married and also when they're separated. We should never be forced to marry. The government has a responsibility to protect us and our family.

- **Article 17:** Everyone has the right to own property, and no one has the right to take this away from us without a fair reason.

- **Article 18:** Everyone has the freedom to think or believe what they want, including the right to religious belief. We have the right to change our beliefs or religion at any time, and the right to publicly or privately practise our chosen religion, alone or with others.

- **Article 19:** Everyone has the right to their own opinions, and to be able to express them freely. We should have the right to share our ideas with who we want, and in whichever way we choose.

- **Article 20:** We should all have the right to form groups and organise peaceful meetings. Nobody should be forced to belong to a group if they don't want to.

- **Article 21:** We all have the right to take part in our country's political affairs either by freely choosing politicians to represent us, or by belonging to the government ourselves. Governments should be voted for by the public on a regular basis, and every person's individual vote should be secret. Every individual vote should be worth the same.

- **Article 22:** The society we live in should help every person develop to their best ability through access to work, involvement in cultural activity, and the right to social welfare. Every person in society should have the freedom to develop their personality with the support of the resources available in that country.

- **Article 23:** We all have the right to employment, to be free to choose our work, and to be paid a fair salary that allows us to live and support our family. Everyone who does the same work should have the right to equal pay, without discrimination. We have the right to come together and form trade union groups to defend our interests as workers.

- **Article 24:** Everyone has the right to rest and leisure time. There should be limits on working hours, and people should be able to take holidays with pay.

- **Article 25:** We all have the right to enough food, clothing, housing, and healthcare for ourselves and our families. We should have access to support if we are out of work, ill, elderly, disabled, widowed, or can't earn a living for reasons outside of our control. An expectant mother and her baby should both receive extra care and support. All children should have the same rights when they are born.

- **Article 26:** Everyone has the right to education. Primary schooling should be free. We should all be able to continue our studies as far as we wish. At school we should be helped to develop our talents, and be taught an understanding and respect for everyone's human rights. We should also be taught to get on with others whatever their ethnicity, religion, or country they come from. Our parents have the right to choose what kind of school we go to.

- **Article 27:** We all have the right to get involved in our community's arts, music, literature, and sciences, and the benefits they bring. If we are an artist, a musician, a writer, or a scientist, our works should be protected and we should be able to benefit from them.

- **Article 28:** We all have the right to live in a peaceful and orderly society so that these rights and freedoms can be protected, and these rights can be enjoyed in all other countries around the world.

- **Article 29:** We have duties to the community we live in that should allow us to develop as fully as possible. The law should guarantee human rights and should allow everyone to enjoy the same mutual respect.

- **Article 30:** No government, group, or individual should act in a way that would destroy the rights and freedoms of the Universal Declaration of Human Rights.

7 December 2023

The above information is reprinted with kind permission from Amnesty International UK.
© Amnesty International UK 2024

www.amnesty.org.uk

Human rights: a legacy of the Holocaust

For International Human Rights Day, Debora Singer MBE, Safeguarding Human Rights Lead at René Cassin, explains how the Jewish community has shaped human rights following the Holocaust, and how our freedoms are currently under threat in the UK.

By Deborah Singer

Human rights have a legacy which the Jewish community holds very dear. The concept of human rights, such as the rights of individuals to not be oppressed by the state, to protest, to speak freely, and to seek protection from persecution, didn't come from nowhere. It came from one of the biggest infringements on human rights within living memory.

When René Cassin, the Jewish voice for human rights, campaigns alongside allies like Friends of the Earth, Liberty, Just Fair, and many others, we have something additional to contribute. When we oppose the Illegal Migration Act, which removes the right to protection from persecution, or the now abandoned Bill of Rights, which would have weakened the Human Rights Act, it's personal. Because human rights are a result of the Holocaust.

How the Jewish community has championed human rights

When Jewish Polish lawyer Hersch Lauterpacht wrote his book *An International Bill of the Rights of Man* in 1945, his most innovative idea was placing the protection of the individual at the centre of international legal order. He included the right to liberty, freedom of religion, of speech, of association and assembly, and privacy of the home. These are all freedoms that had been denied to minorities by the Nazis, people like Jews, Gypsies and Roma, gay people, disabled people, and Communists.

Lauterpacht's work was informed by his legal training and experience as a professor of international law at Cambridge University. But it was also informed by the fact that, except for one niece, he lost all his family in the Holocaust.

The Universal Declaration of Human Rights was co-written by a Jewish lawyer, Monsieur René Cassin. A French jurist, he drew on Lauterpacht's work when putting together the document that was adopted by the United Nations in 1948. It was the first time that a community of nations had made a declaration of human rights and freedoms.

Like Lauterpacht, Monsieur René Cassin lost most of his family members to the Holocaust. He himself had to flee to safety in London during the war. The belief that never again should a state be able to perpetuate such gross human rights violations on its own citizens with impunity was recognised internationally. But it's not a surprise that it was Jewish lawyers, who had themselves been directly affected by the Holocaust, who led on the thinking and development of international human rights frameworks.

The European Convention on Human Rights differs from the Universal Declaration as it has an accountability mechanism, a court in Strasbourg where people can take their cases if their convention rights are breached. Although it was written by David Maxwell Fyfe, a British Conservative politician, with the support of Winston Churchill, Lauterpacht's influence is seen heavily in its drafting. Indeed, Maxwell Fyfe stated that 'I had the good fortune to have Lauterpacht's personal help when I was preparing the European Convention on Human Rights.'

On developing the European Court of Human Rights in Strasbourg, British barrister John Harcourt Barrington stated, 'We shamelessly borrowed many ideas from Hersch Lauterpacht's framework of the rights of man.'

In the UK, the European Convention was brought into domestic law by the Labour government with the support of all the major political parties. Jewish legal policy expert Francesca Klug was the government's adviser on this and was therefore central to the creation of the Human Rights Act 1998.

How human rights are at risk in the UK

We all benefit from the Human Rights Act. Whether as people of faith who are able to wear our religious symbols to work, women escaping violent partners who are able to access housing for themselves and their children, or elderly couples who are able to stay together at the end of their lives, the Human Rights Act is the recourse.

Alongside our allies, we fought off the Bill of Rights. But now the European Convention is under threat from some senior Conservatives, most notably former Home Secretary Suella Braverman. Similarly, the UN's Refugee Convention is also being questioned.

In arguing for the preservation of the Refugee Convention and against the Illegal Migration Act, we make the point that the Refugee Convention is a response to the Holocaust. Many in the Jewish community themselves fled or have parents or grandparents who fled Nazi Europe. The Refugee Convention was written in 1951 to ensure that states take responsibility for those fleeing persecution. The Illegal Migration Act removes this right to state protection.

When we consider this, we think of our relatives who couldn't get out of Nazi Europe. We need the Refugee Convention to ensure that those seeking protection have a right to claim asylum in another country. We feel extremely strongly about the current government's anti-refugee rhetoric and about the appalling conditions for those seeking asylum. The environmental movement is right to join with us in defending these rights, and to raise the increasing plight of climate refugees.

Two of the key conventions that came out of the Holocaust, the European Convention on Human Rights, and the Refugee Convention, are now under threat in the UK. The rights of individuals to freedoms and protection are at risk.

As a Jewish human rights organisation, we're proud to campaign with partners such as Friends of the Earth to maintain our human rights treaties. Because we all have the right to fairness, dignity, and respect.

Alongside allies such as René Cassin, Friends of the Earth is defending our hard-fought rights to have our voices heard and demand climate action.

7 December 2023

Activity

Answer the following questions:

1. Who wrote *An International Bill of the Rights of Man*?
2. Which rights were included in the book?
3. Who was René Cassin?
4. How did the Holocaust influence human rights?
5. Where is the European Court of Human Rights?
6. Are our human rights under threat? If so, how?
7. Who benefits from the Human Rights Act?
8. When was the Human Rights Act created?

Research

Do some research on René Cassin and write a short biography.

Research

When was the Refugee Convention introduced? How does the Illegal Migration Act contradict it?

The above information is reprinted with kind permission from Friends of the Earth.
© 2024 Friends of the Earth Limited

www.friendsoftheearth.uk

5 Ways the European Convention on Human Rights makes the UK a better place

We all want to live in a society where everyone is treated with dignity and respect. The European Convention on Human Rights helps us towards this dream. Here's how.

1. The ECHR puts your basic rights into law

The European Convention on Human Rights (often shortened to just ECHR) was drafted in the aftermath of the Second World War and the Holocaust.

Its goal was to make sure the atrocities committed would never be repeated, by declaring the basic rights and freedoms of every single person which must be respected and protected by the State.

The United Kingdom played an important role in the birth of the convention. Winston Churchill was a driving force behind it, and British lawyers were key to drafting the text.

The ECHR came into force 70 years ago on 3 September 1953, guaranteeing everyone's fundamental rights in law for the first time.

2. The ECHR protects every single person in the UK

The United Kingdom was one of the first states to sign up to the ECHR way back in 1951.

The very first part of the document (Article 1) makes clear that States that sign up to it pledge to respect the convention rights of 'everyone within their jurisdiction'.

This means the ECHR protects every single person in the UK. Not just a privileged few. Not just British citizens. Everyone.

Our rights are interconnected – either everyone has human rights, or no one does. There is no in-between and states can't lawfully remove human rights from one group of people.

All the rights and freedoms we are familiar with come from the ECHR.

It protects all of us from things like torture, unlawful killing, and slavery, and guarantees our freedom of speech, assembly, religion, privacy, and much more.

3. The ECHR empowers you to challenge abuse of your rights

As we've already noted, states that have signed up to the ECHR have pledged to respect everyone's rights.

And the European Court of Human Rights exists to enforce this if a state fails.

There have been several cases where the Court has protected and even advanced human rights in the UK.

- Freedom of expression for the press comes from a case known as Sunday Times from 1979.
- The decriminalisation of homosexual acts in Northern Ireland came about thanks to a case called Dudgeon from 1981.

- A case called Smith and Grady made clear that banning LGBT+ people from serving in the Armed Forces breaches human rights.
- A Liberty case known as Eweida, said the state has to make sure private companies respect the religious freedom of their employees.
- A case called Goodwin made clear the state has a duty to provide disabled people with appropriate care.

The list goes on.

And the ECHR is capable of changing with the times – it's what is known as a 'living instrument'. For example, a case called Goodwin established the right to change a person's legal gender in the UK.

4. The ECHR led to our Human Rights Act

Our Human Rights Act incorporates the convention rights into UK law.

The HRA (as it's known for short) forces public authorities – like government departments, local councils, the police, and hospitals – to put measures in place to respect your rights. These are known as 'positive obligations'. And if public authorities fall short, the HRA empowers you to challenge them in British courts, rather than having to go all the way to the European Court.

These positive obligations mean the Human Rights Act is protecting all of us, every day, and it's unlikely you will ever have to start a legal case to defend your rights.

Just like the convention, the HRA applies to everyone equally.

When making new laws, our Human Rights Act also requires the government to ensure proposals do not breach your rights. And in court cases, judges have to interpret laws in a way that respects your rights.

5. The ECHR helps secure peace in Northern Ireland

The Convention is baked into the Northern Ireland peace process.

The Good Friday Agreement of 1998 was a historical deal supported by both the North and South of Ireland that brought an end to the violence of the Troubles.

The Agreement placed a duty on the UK Government to incorporate the ECHR into Northern Irish law so that people could challenge injustice in the courts if their rights were breached.

This was achieved through our Human Rights Act, which – as we've said – forces public authorities to respect your rights, and gives you the power to challenge them in court if they don't.

The European Convention on Human Rights is one of the great humanitarian achievements, helping to keep everyone in the UK safe and free.

Liberty will always support and fight to protect the UK's membership of the ECHR.

30 August 2023

The above information is reprinted with kind permission from Liberty.
© 2024 Liberty

www.libertyhumanrights.org.uk

Chapter 2

Human Rights Today

From Gaza to Ukraine, what would the pioneers of human rights think of our world today?

The 1948 Universal Declaration of Human Rights protects the most vulnerable: we must fight to defend and extend it.

By Philippe Sands

During the week when we mark 75 years of the Universal Declaration of Human Rights and the 1948 Convention on the Prevention and Punishment of Genocide, I have been thinking about the genesis of both events and how we should commemorate them now.

Adopted within 24 hours of each other in Paris in December 1948, the Universal Declaration seeks to protect individuals, while the Convention seeks to protect groups. That moment in Paris was revolutionary: a recognition that the rights of the state are not unlimited, that the days of being allowed as a matter of law to trample over human lives were over.

How does it feel? I go back to that period around 1945, to the publication of two books, by two men whose origins and ideas may be traced to the remarkable city of Lviv, and to the law faculty of its university. One was *Axis Rule in Occupied Europe* by Rafael Lemkin, published in November 1944, in which he coined the word 'genocide.' The other is *An International Bill of the Rights of Man* by Hersch Lauterpacht, published a few months later, in which he set out the ideas that would inform the development of human rights and 'crimes against humanity.'

Both men were part of the prosecution teams at Nuremberg. They prosecuted Hans Frank, who once served as Adolf Hitler's lawyer, unaware that he was involved in the murder of their entire families. This they only learned at the end of the trial. It would be understandable if both men had curled up in a corner and wept, about the state of the world, about the loss of their families. They didn't. They developed ideas, then they pushed those ideas. How would they feel today, 75 years on?

How would they feel about the rights of the writer Victoria Amelina, my friend, and all the other civilians killed in Ukraine? How would they feel about the rights of the Chagossians, forcibly deported from their homes 50 years ago, and still not able to return? How would they feel about a British government that seeks to limit the effect of the European Convention on Human Rights – drafted with significant input from the UK – to allow the country to send people to Rwanda, a place that the Supreme Court has determined not to be safe? How would they feel about the terrible deaths that occurred in southern Israel on 7 October 2023? How would they feel about the terrible deaths that have followed in Gaza? How would they feel about the mass incarceration of the Uyghurs? How would they feel about the policy of torture embraced after September 11?

We can speculate, but we cannot know. But I know how I feel, on this anniversary, inspired by their ideas and endeavours and those of countless others. I would say: this is not a moment of celebration, but of recognition, of how much remains to be done, and also of what is different today and what we have.

Four years ago, I was on a panel at George Washington University with Thomas Buergenthal, a former judge at the international Court of Justice. Many decades earlier, as a 10-year-old boy, he was in the care of a medical doctor named Josef Mengele, at a place called Auschwitz. The panel we shared was a week before the hearings in The Hague in the case brought by the Gambia against Myanmar, an application for provisional measures to stop the genocide of the Rohingya. 'Can you imagine,' said Tom, 'if in 1944 there had been a treaty which said you could not treat people as I and others were treated, and a court of judges to which countries could go, and a faraway country that would actually be willing to go to that court and ask the judges to order that such behaviour must stop?'

At the hearing in The Hague a week later, I found myself sitting alongside Aung San Suu Kyi, who appeared as agent for Myanmar. I did not find myself in agreement with much she said that day, but one sentence she spoke has remained with me: 'International law may well be our only global value system.'

And so it was. The 17 judges acted unanimously to adopt a far-reaching provisional measures order, with unprecedented reporting requirements. In Cox's Bazar, in Bangladesh, hundreds of Rohingya refugees stood and held up placards, on which three words were written: 'Thank you Gambia.'

So, 75 years on, how should we mark the anniversaries of the universal declaration and the convention? We may not have enough, but we have more than nothing, and that allows hope and a block on which to build.

Four things come to mind in these dismal times, in this lawless world in which we must recognise the limits of what has been achieved.

One: Protect what we have, what was achieved in that remarkable moment in 1948, for it – and the ideals of the rule of law – are under grievous threat right now.

Two: Build on accountability for all. Support the international Law Commission convention on crimes against humanity. Support accountability for all international crimes, including the crime of aggression. Support an international criminal court (ICC) that holds everyone to account, not just the weakest or those who happen to be from Africa.

Three: Move beyond the rights of the human and embrace the rights of nature. On climate, the scientists tell us that what is coming fast will be catastrophic, that the failure of Cop28 to commit to phasing out fossil fuels will be inadequate. Perhaps the environment will be fine, but we humans will not be. Think about rights in relation to the climate crisis. Think about ecocide, to be added to the ICC statute as the fifth international crime.

Four: Act on the continuing effects of historic wrongdoing, not least enslavement and colonialism – which Emmanuel Macron characterised as a 'crime against humanity' – and historic emissions of greenhouse gases. You may not like it, but reparation, or something akin to it, is on the table and it's here to stay.

Philippe Sands is Professor of Law at University College London and author of East West Street: On the Origins of Genocide and Crimes against Humanity

12 December 2023

Define

- Write a short definition of the word 'genocide'.
- Write a short definition of the word 'ecocide'.

The above information is reprinted with kind permission from *The Guardian*.
© 2024 Guardian News and Media Limited

www.theguardian.com

People's rights are threatened everywhere, from wars to silence about abuses, rights group says

A leading human rights group says people's rights are being suppressed and threatened everywhere in the world, from wars to selective outrage about some abuses and silence about others.

By Edith M. Lederer

People's rights are being suppressed and threatened everywhere in the world, from wars to selective government outrage about some abuses and silence about others because of 'political expediency,' a leading human rights group said Thursday (11 January 2024).

'We only have to look at the human rights challenges of 2023 to tell us what we need to do differently in 2024,' Human Rights Watch said in its annual global report.

Armed conflicts have mushroomed, leading with the Israel-Hamas war, and the issue is how governments respond to them, Tirana Hassan, the rights group's Executive Director, told a news conference. 'It needs to be an end to double standards.'

As an example, she said many governments quickly and justifiably condemned the 'unlawful' killings and atrocities by Hamas when it attacked southern Israel on 7 October 2023, killing hundreds and taking hostages. After the attacks, Israel 'unlawfully blocked' aid to Gaza residents and its ongoing offensive in the territory has killed more than 23,000 people, according to the Gaza Health Ministry, while reducing entire neighbourhoods to rubble.

'Yet many of the governments that condemned Hamas' war crimes have been muted in responding to the war crimes committed by the Israeli government,' Hassan said.

She said such selective outrage sends a dangerous message that some people's lives matter more than others and shakes the legitimacy of the international rules that protect everyone's human rights.

Human Rights Watch praised South Africa for seeking a ruling from the International Court of Justice on whether Israel is committing genocide in Gaza in a landmark case that began Thursday. Hassan said other countries including the United States should support South Africa's action 'and ensure that Israel complies with the court's decision.'

The report said tradeoffs on human rights in the name of politics are also clear. It cited the failure of many governments to speak out about the Chinese government's repression and control over civil society, the internet and media.

'Chinese authorities' cultural persecution and arbitrary detention of a million Uyghurs and other Turkic Muslims amount to crimes against humanity,' it said. 'Yet many governments, including in predominantly Muslim countries, stay silent.'

The report described the US and European Union as ignoring their human rights obligations in favor of politically expedient solutions.

'US President Joe Biden has shown little appetite to hold responsible human rights abusers who are key to his domestic agenda or are seen as bulwarks to China,' it said.

'US allies like Saudi Arabia, India, and Egypt violate the rights of their people on a massive scale yet have not had to overcome hurdles to deepen their ties with the US,' the report said. 'Vietnam, the Philippines, India, and other nations the US wants as counters to China have been feted at the White House without regard for their human rights abuses at home.'

Human Rights Watch said the European Union circumvents its human rights obligations to asylum seekers and migrants, 'especially those from Africa and the Middle East, striking deals with abusive governments like Libya, Turkey and Tunisia to keep migrants outside of the European bloc.'

Several national leaders were named as examples of worrying trends. India's 'democracy has slid toward autocracy' under Prime Minister Narendra Modi, Tunisia's President Kais Saied has weakened the judiciary and El Salvador's President Nayib Bukele has used mass detention as an ostensible solution for fighting crime, the report said.

The group cited as a bright spot for the year the International Criminal Court's arrest warrants for Russian President Vladimir Putin and his children's rights commissioner, alleging war crimes related to the forced transfer of Ukrainian children from Russian-occupied areas, and their deportation to Russia.

Hassan also pointed to the movement toward marriage equality in places like Nepal but especially to the determination of Afghan girls and women who took to the streets to oppose the Taliban bans on work and education and have found alternative ways to learn.

'If the people at the center whose human rights are being abused are still prepared to fight then human rights matter,' she said.

12 January 2024

The above information is reprinted with kind permission from *The Independent*.
© independent.co.uk 2024

www.independent.co.uk

issues: Human Rights   Chapter 2: Human Rights Today

The universality of human rights needs defending

Seventy-five years on from the adoption of the Universal Declaration of Human Rights, its promise of freedom and equality remains a distant dream for those living under religious rule, says Stephen Evans.

This Sunday (10th December) will mark the 75th anniversary of the Universal Declaration of Human Rights (UDHR). Created in response to the horrors of the Second World War, the Declaration is regarded by some as one of humanity's greatest achievements. Its articulation of a common vision of respectful and peaceful coexistence has underpinned human rights treaties across the globe and inspired many individuals and policymakers to work towards a better world.

One of the key principles of human rights is universality – the idea that human beings are endowed with equal rights simply by virtue of being human, wherever they live and whoever they are, regardless of their status or any particular characteristics. Critics of the notion of universality often dismiss such rights as 'Western values' emanating from a European, Judeo-Christian or Enlightenment heritage. The concept of universality is receiving increasing pushback, particularly from religious groups who want to redraw the boundaries of human rights in line with 'cultural and intellectual traditions'. But as the former UN Special Rapporteur on freedom of religion or belief Ahmed Shaheed has articulated, claims that human rights are a Western concept fail to recognise the major influence of non-Western states in the drafting of the UDHR, and fall flat when looking back at historical global support for human rights.

Yet one thing is certain: human rights are not universally applied today. One of the biggest barriers to the flourishing of rights is religion, particularly where it enjoys proximity to political power. It's no coincidence that the world's theocracies – Afghanistan, Iran, Mauritania, Saudi Arabia and Yemen, for example – are amongst the world's worst human rights violators. Freedom of expression has been a particular bugbear of majority Muslim nations. Between 1999 and 2010, a coalition of 57 Islamic nations known as the Organisation of Islamic Cooperation (OIC) launched a concerted effort to limit free speech around religion globally. The OIC pushed 'defamation of religion' resolutions at the United Nations, arguing that Muslims were facing growing intolerance and discrimination, which they described as 'Islamophobia.' But their attempts to curtail speech were more about protecting religion than individuals.

The campaign by Islamic nations faced opposition from Western democracies, which argued that 'defamation of religion' resolutions would violate the right to freedom of speech, thought, conscience, and religion. Eventually the defamation approach was abandoned but attempts to restrict free speech around Islam continue through the contested concept of 'Islamophobia' and the utilisation of 'hate speech' resolutions at the UN to protect religious feelings.

Freedom of expression is far from the only human right that vexes religious fundamentalists. Since Afghanistan fell back into a theocratic government, the Taliban have imposed their strict and brutal interpretation of Islam, flagrantly flouting numerous human rights principles with total disregard for international law. According to Human Rights Watch, since taking power the Taliban have imposed rules that comprehensively prevent women and girls from exercising their most fundamental rights to expression, movement, and education, and affect their other basic rights to life,

issues: Human Rights   17   Chapter 2: Human Rights Today

livelihood, healthcare, food and water. They have prohibited women from travelling abroad or going to their workplace without a male family member accompanying them, and barred them from many jobs. Almost all girls are denied access to secondary school. This amounts to the almost total exclusion of half the population – women and girls – from public life.

In Iran, where Islamic clerics brutally impose their religion on the population, women have been at the forefront of movements to see the suffocating and repressive regime replaced with a free, open, and modern secular state. The most recent wave of protests led by women and girls chanting 'Woman, Life, Freedom' were sparked by the death of Mahsa Amini, who died in police custody following her arrest for her alleged non-compliance with the country's Islamic dress code, which mandates women to wear the hijab in public places.

It's been a rude awakening for the mullahs who claim so-called 'Western' values aren't universal. They're finding out that liberal values of separation of religion and state, free expression, equality, and freedom of and from religion are more universal than they thought. The regime's response has been mass arrests, extreme and excessive violence, and public executions. More than 500 people, including 71 children, were killed in the protests.

Those living under theocracies understand the need for secularism better than most. The concept of universality resonates most strongly with those who are marginalised or experience discrimination. Children, LGBT+ people, religious minorities, and women bear the brunt whenever religious fundamentalists can impose their will on societies.

The 2022 US Supreme Court ruling in Roe v Wade was a wake-up call to the global threat conservative religious views pose to women's reproductive rights. Closer to home an ascendant religious right is eroding reproductive freedoms in Italy and Poland. The UK is not immune from attempts to restrict women's ability to have legal abortions. Three 'pro-life' Private Members' bills are being introduced to the House of Lords in a bid to do just that.

LGBT+ people's human rights are being restricted by religiously motivated policies, laws and practices that discriminate or fuel prejudice against them. Children's education is impeded by attempts to indoctrinate. The Convention on the Rights of the Child declares that children's right to education should be directed to the 'preparation of the child for responsible life in a free society.' Yet just as hard-line Taliban leaders push for a complete ban on girls' education, fundamentalist religious groups in the UK run unregistered schools where children are denied a secular education and indoctrinated only with religion.

Persistent attempts by religious fundamentalists to impose their interpretation of doctrine on others demonstrates the necessity of secularism. Our mission is to build a freer, fairer, and more tolerant society where people are free to follow the beliefs they choose and where no particular belief systems are privileged or imposed. Only by resisting religious power-seeking can we ensure human rights aren't overridden on the grounds of religion, tradition, or culture.

Believers and nonbelievers alike who want to protect and promote human rights should embrace secularist principles to fend off religious challenges that would fatally and fundamentally undermine them. And we need, more than ever, to protect the fundamental principle that all rights are universal. Let's make sure the 75th anniversary of the UDHR sees renewed efforts to give effect to human rights on the ground for everyone, everywhere.

7 December 2023

The above information is reprinted with kind permission from the National Secular Society.
© National Secular Society 2024

www.secularism.org.uk

The long shadow of Qatar's human rights abuses

By Cathryn Grothe

A spotlight on Qatar

The international spotlight is on Qatar for the 2022 World Cup. It's not only the football matches that are receiving global attention, but also Qatar's harrowing human rights record. To fully appreciate the controversy surrounding this year's host country, it is important to understand the long history of repression.

Qatari citizens only make up about 10% of the population, while the majority of people living in the country are foreign nationals, largely migrant workers from South Asia. This disparity is not uncommon in the Arab Gulf, where migrant workers flock for employment opportunities.

While Qatari citizens are among the wealthiest in the world, the large portion of noncitizens not only earn low wages but also lack the same political rights and civil liberties awarded to Qataris; exploitative foreign labour laws box out noncitizens from realising the same economic opportunities as citizens. This discrimination and labour exploitation was foundational to Qatar's preparations for the World Cup.

The deadly cost of World Cup construction

The Qatari government has spent billions of dollars in infrastructure projects to prepare for the World Cup. These projects, which included constructing stadiums, hotels, highways, and expanding the airport in Doha, largely relied on migrant labour. They also came at a deadly cost.

In recent years, it has become clear that the basic human rights of migrant workers who contributed to World Cup infrastructure projects were significantly violated. Reporting has documented gruelling working conditions, long hours, unclean living situations, and wage-theft. *The Guardian* estimates that thousands of migrant workers have died in Qatar since the country was awarded the World Cup. And, while human rights advocates have been calling on Fédération internationale de football association (FIFA) to provide financial remedies to the families of the deceased, that has yet to be realised.

Unfortunately, this horrific practice of exploiting migrant labour is not new in Qatar. Migrant workers, who make up 90% of the workforce, are constrained by the country's sponsorship system known as the kafala system. This is a colonial-era work visa sponsorship system that still exists in countries such as Jordan, Lebanon, and many Arab Gulf states. The kafala system offers very few protections for labourers and essentially gives employers total control over foreign workers including their wages, ability to travel, and immigration status.

Although Qatar announced major reforms to the kafala system in 2020, these changes in practice fell short of what was promised. Human rights groups began sounding the alarm about the potential for abuse of foreign workers back when Qatar was awarded the right to host the World Cup in 2010. Unfortunately, neither FIFA nor Qatari authorities did much to provide meaningful protections for migrant workers.

A long history of repression

Qatar's history of violating basic human rights extends far beyond labour exploitation. Freedom of expression, press freedoms, and freedom of association are all severely restricted in Qatar, which Freedom House ranks Not Free in *Freedom in the World*, an annual survey of political rights and civil liberties. In fact, Freedom House analysis shows that the human rights situation has not improved, and has in fact declined, since Qatar won the right to host the World Cup back in 2010.

Most print and broadcast media outlets are closely linked to the state and authorities impose tight restrictions on journalists, leaving very little room for independent journalism. Ahead of the World Cup, foreign media outlets were informed that they would need special permission to speak with locals, a clear effort by authorities to control the narrative around the event.

Those who are critical of the state, including activists and journalists, have received incredibly harsh prison sentences often following unfair trials. These practices encourage self-censorship and significantly undermine any space for free expression. Recently, a criminal court in Qatar handed down life sentences to several human rights activists simply for their involvement in peaceful protests.

Discriminatory laws significantly limit the civil liberties of women, religious minorities, and LGBT+ people. For example, the male guardianship system requires women to get permission from male guardians to exercise basic rights such as get an education, marry, travel abroad, and access reproductive healthcare.

Similarly, LGBT+ people living in Qatar face extreme discrimination and harassment. Qatar's Penal Code criminalises a range of consensual same-sex sexual acts and includes jail terms for those found guilty. While Qatari authorities have said everyone will be welcome at the World Cup, regardless of their background, reports of discrimination against match attendees based on their LGBT+ expression have already emerged.

Don't let up the pressure after the games end

Qatar is not the first repressive regime to host a major international sporting or cultural event, and it likely won't be the last. China hosted the Winter Olympics while committing acts of genocide against the Uyghur people in Xinjiang. Russia hosted the 2018 World Cup under the same regime that is currently waging a brutal war against its democratic neighbour of Ukraine. While not a host, Iran has made its authoritarian mark on the games through the silencing of its players who dared to show solidarity with protesters in Tehran and through harassing and threatening the families of players.

Those following the World Cup, including democratic leaders in attendance and businesses sponsoring the event, must not ignore the ugly scene taking place behind the spectacle of the beautiful game. The abuses happening in the country – against women, LGBT+ individuals, migrant workers, and other marginalised populations – demand our continued attention long after the last goal is scored.

7 December 2022

Key Facts

- 90% of the workforce for the Qatar World Cup were migrant workers.
- Freedom House ranks Qatar as Not Free in the *Freedom in the World* survey.
- Qatar handed down life sentences to several human rights activists simply for their involvement in peaceful protests.
- Media is heavily censored and there are tight restrictions on journalists.
- The male guardianship system requires women to get permission from male guardians to exercise basic rights such as get an education, marry, travel abroad, and access reproductive healthcare.
- LGBT+ people living in Qatar face extreme discrimination and harassment.

The above information is reprinted with kind permission from the Democracy Paradox.
© 2024 Democracy Paradox

www.democracyparadox.com

Qatar World Cup workers suffered 'human rights abuses', new Amnesty report finds

The investigation showed a 'pattern of abuses against migrant workers' and accused FIFA of failing to investigate the issue, writes Miguel Delaney

Hundreds of security guards and marshals at the Qatar World Cup went unpaid for long working periods without days off, before being forced out of the country when the tournament ended, a new Amnesty International investigation has found. Some did not earn enough to pay off the loan required for recruitment costs.

The human rights body states that research into Teyseer Security Services 'shows [a] pattern of abuses against migrant workers.' Steve Cockburn, Amnesty's Head of Economic and Social Justice, has meanwhile accused FIFA of failing 'to effectively investigate the issue or offer remedies,' demanding that the global governing body step in and 'offer immediate and meaningful remediation for the human rights abuses suffered by workers'.

The group spoke to 22 men from Nepal, Kenya, and Ghana, who were among thousands of migrant workers employed on short-term contracts by Qatar-based Teyseer Security Services to work as marshals and security guards at World Cup sites in the build-up and during the tournament itself. Among the locations were Khalifa International Stadium, FIFA fan zones, the Corniche, and the metro station in Souk Waqif.

All of the workers interviewed said 'false promises' were made by either Teyseer's representatives or recruitment agents, among them the suggestions they could take up more senior roles to earn an extra £220 a month, or stay and work in the country beyond the three-month contract period. Once in Qatar, however, nothing materialised.

Instead, a third of those interviewed – particularly those employed as marshals – said they had to work 12 hours every day for 28 consecutive days. That came without any day off or adequate pay to reflect this work, which breaches Qatari law. The work often involved standing for long hours without sitting down and dealing with large crowds without adequate training or support.

'I had to take out a loan to pay for the expenses to travel to work in Qatar during the World Cup,' Marcus, his name changed at his request, told Amnesty. 'I am still paying it, what I earned was not enough.'

Richard, who has also requested his name be changed and worked at one of the team training grounds, found he would have earned more had he stayed in Ghana.

'I lost because I paid almost £550 before going there. I only received about £1,200, so I only made £650. I would get more than that if I had stayed in Ghana. I lost my job as a result [of going] so I came back with little money and no job.'

Kiran, a changed name for a worker from Nepal, found the nature of his work at the Souk Waqif metro intimidating and physically arduous.

'It was a tough job because there was one metro [station] in the area and too much of a crowd. I had to stand for ten

to 12 hours a day… just resting my back on the barricades. At times we felt scared because it was too busy, and people were pushing.'

Cockburn puts the primary responsibility on FIFA and Qatar, stating the country's existing mechanism for redress is 'not fit for purpose.'

He said: 'The World Cup organisers were well aware of the issues but failed to put in place adequate measures to protect workers and prevent predictable labour abuses at World Cup sites, even after workers raised these issues directly.

'It's six months since the tournament concluded but FIFA and Qatar have yet to offer an effective and accessible scheme to enable abused workers to receive the justice and compensation they are owed. Qatar's existing mechanism for redress is not fit for purpose and has left thousands of workers deprived of compensation for the abuses they suffered.

'FIFA has a clear responsibility to ensure human rights are respected throughout the supply chain engaged in preparing and delivering its showcase competition.

'Although six months have passed since the World Cup, FIFA has yet to effectively investigate the issue, or offer remedies. Workers have already waited too long for justice. FIFA must now step in and offer immediate and meaningful remediation for the human rights abuses suffered by workers.'

The abuses led many of Teyseer's workers to protest on multiple occasions while they were in Qatar. Some told Amnesty they reported their treatment on the World Cup Grievances Hotline but no action was taken.

'I had to take out a loan to pay for the expenses to travel to work in Qatar during the World Cup … I am still paying it, what I earned was not enough.'

One said a manager threatened to fire him in relation to complaining and warned him not to report issues again. Hundreds of marshals eventually staged a protest demanding their dues days before their contracts expired in January, after which workers said representatives of both Teyseer and the government promised they would be compensated. That has not yet been honoured.

Teyseer representatives threatened 'action' if the men failed to leave Qatar on flights arranged by the company. Hundreds had to leave Qatar without compensation.

Teyseer denied the allegations to Amnesty, saying the company followed an 'ethical recruitment process' while detailing various measures it had taken to protect workers' rights. FIFA told Amnesty due diligence was conducted on the security firm but there were 'different perceptions and views' on the experience of workers.

The global governing body said it would seek further clarification on the issues raised but did not offer commitment to provide remedy.

Qatar has introduced a grievance mechanism but workers must still be in the country to access the state's labour courts and any compensation scheme. There is no way to complain remotely and, with workers inevitably forced to leave once their contracts are up, Amnesty state they have been 'denied justice'.

The Qatari government repeated the common line to Amnesty that measures had been taken in recent years to reform its labour system.

Amnesty conclude by stating that the abuses endured are 'part of a pattern suffered by migrant workers in Qatar' since the decision was taken to award the state the World Cup in 2010.

In a statement to *The Independent*, FIFA said: 'FIFA, in collaboration with its Qatari counterparts, implemented a far-reaching due diligence process with the aim to ensure that companies involved in FIFA World Cup-related construction and services abide by the Supreme Committee's (SC) Workers' Welfare Standards. We consider any non-compliance with these standards unacceptable and are actively following up when we learn about alleged breaches.

'After receiving Amnesty International's allegations concerning Teyseer's workers on 19 April 2023, FIFA promptly followed up with the SC's Workers Welfare Department (WWD) as well as with the Doha Office of the International Labour Organization (ILO). It is the primary responsibility of the respective companies as well as the Qatari authorities to rectify possible adverse impacts on workers. As FIFA, we work to use our leverage with the relevant entities to promote the provision of remedy when we become aware of such allegations, in line with our responsibilities under international standards.

'We kindly refer you to the SC and the ILO for further information on this case.

'More broadly, one should not lose track of the bigger picture: International experts and trade union representatives who have assessed and collaborated in the labour rights programme for FIFA World Cup workers have repeatedly recognised that it led to heightened protection and welfare for FIFA World Cup workers.

'In addition, according to the International Labour Organization, Qatar's labour reforms have been significant and benefitted hundreds of thousands of workers with the World Cup being an important catalyst for these reforms. It is undeniable that significant progress has taken place, and it is equally clear that the enforcement of such transformative reforms takes time and that heightened efforts are needed to ensure the reforms benefit all workers in the country.'

15 June 2023

Write

The 2030 FIFA World Cup will be the 24th FIFA World Cup.

Imagine that the host had not yet been announced, but that one of the countries that was bidding to hold the competition had a bad record for human rights. Write a letter to FIFA to try to dissuade them from choosing that country.

Use persuasive language to get your point across to show FIFA the impact that it would have on the reputation of FIFA should they support a host that abuses human rights.

The above information is reprinted with kind permission from *The Independent*.
© independent.co.uk 2024

www.independent.co.uk

issues: Human Rights — Chapter 2: Human Rights Today

World Cup: FIFA must press for binding human rights commitments from 2030 and 2034 hosts

- **Saudi Arabia is the only bidder for 2034, while Morocco/Portugal/Spain is the sole 2030 bid.**

- **A lack of competition to host tournaments risks undermining FIFA's leverage, warns Sport & Rights Alliance.**

- **'Human rights commitments must be agreed with potential hosts before final decisions on holding the tournaments are made' – Steve Cockburn**

FIFA needs to secure clear and binding commitments to improve human rights in countries likely to host the 2030 and 2034 men's football World Cup tournaments to prevent serious potential abuses linked to its flagship event, the Sport & Rights Alliance said today.

The group's warning comes as Saudi Arabia has become the sole bidder to host the 2034 event shortly before the deadline for bids closes at midnight tonight, while a joint bid from Morocco, Portugal, and Spain is currently the only one being considered for 2030.

The Sport & Rights Alliance – a coalition of human rights and anti-corruption organisations, trade unions, fans representatives, athlete survivors groups, and players unions – believes the lack of competition to host the tournaments risks undermining FIFA's leverage, meaning it is crucial that football's world governing body takes the lead and secures binding human rights guarantees from the bidders.

The bidding process for the 2030 World Cup had been expected to be officially launched at a FIFA Council meeting in June, but was postponed to 'ensure additional consultation with all key stakeholders.' In a surprise move on 4 October, the FIFA Council announced that the only bid to be considered for the 2030 World Cup would be that of Morocco, Portugal and Spain – with a small number of games to be played in Argentina, Paraguay, and Uruguay, which had previously announced their intention to bid to host the entire tournament.

At the same October meeting, FIFA also unexpectedly announced that the bidding process for the 2034 World Cup would begin immediately, with only bids from Asia and Oceania to be considered. With potential bidders given a deadline of just 27 days to declare their intention, only Saudi Arabia has done so.

According to guidelines published by FIFA, any countries bidding to host the 2030 or 2034 World Cups must commit to 'respecting internationally recognised human rights' and 'requires human rights and labour standards to be implemented by the bidding member associations, the government(s), and other entities involved in the organisation of the competitions.'

As part of their official bids, countries must undertake and publish an independent human rights risk assessment and submit a plan that outlines how key risks identified will be addressed. Such risks could include, for example, abuses of workers' rights, forced evictions, discrimination, restrictions on freedom of expression, or corruption.

It is essential that FIFA ensures that human rights risk assessments are genuinely independent. In past processes, bidding football associations have been able to propose who conducts these assessments, leaving the exercise vulnerable to potential bias or abuse.

If FIFA were to fully implement its own policies, bids that are evaluated as being 'high risk' could theoretically be rejected, or corrective plans agreed. In any case, FIFA should ensure continual dialogue with the Sport & Rights Alliance to identify risks and ways to avoid and overcome them.

An opinion poll of more than 17,000 people in 15 countries published by Amnesty in June 2023 showed that a majority of fans wanted human rights standards to be a key consideration when selecting the host of a major sports event such as the World Cup.

Steve Cockburn, Amnesty International's Head of Economic and Social Justice, said:

'With only a single bid for each tournament on the table, FIFA may have scored an own goal.

'FIFA must now make clear how it expects hosts to comply with its human rights policies,

'It must also be prepared to halt the bidding process if serious human rights risks are not credibly addressed,

'The best chance for FIFA to obtain binding guarantees to protect workers' rights, ensure freedom of expression and prevent discrimination linked to the World Cup is during the host selection process – not after the hosts have been confirmed and tournament preparation has begun,

'Human rights commitments must be agreed with potential hosts before final decisions on holding the tournaments are made.'

Minky Worden, Director of Global Initiatives at Human Rights Watch, said:

'Given the enormous scale of the World Cup, there are far-reaching human rights risks to consider with all bids to host this tournament - as well as opportunities for change that should not be missed,

'FIFA's human rights policy must not be reduced to a paper exercise when it comes to choosing the host of the world's most watched sporting event.'

Ronan Evain, Executive Director of Football Supporters Europe, said:

'FIFA's failure in 2010 to insist on human rights protections when it awarded the 2022 World Cup to Qatar is a major reason why serious reforms were so delayed, and so often weakly implemented and enforced,

'FIFA is now required under its own human rights rules to take these lessons seriously and take firm action. It would be a first step to salvage the already tarnished reputations of 2030 and 2034 World Cups with supporters.'

Sport & Rights Alliance

The Sport & Rights Alliance partners include Amnesty International, The Army of Survivors, Committee to Protect Journalists, Football Supporters Europe, Human Rights Watch, ILGA World (the International Lesbian, Gay, Bisexual, Trans, and Intersex Association), the International Trade Union Confederation, and World Players Association, UNI Global Union.

31 October 2023

Debate

As a class, debate the 2034 World Cup being held in Saudi Arabia. One half of the class will be for Saudi Arabia acting as hosts and the other half against them being host.

Research

Create a survey asking participants views on whether or not human rights should be taken into account when deciding where sporting events take place.

The above information is reprinted with kind permission from Amnesty International UK.
© Amnesty International UK 2024

www.amnesty.org.uk

What is modern slavery?

You might think that slavery is a thing of the past. But right now, almost 50 million people are trapped in slavery worldwide.

It's a problem that affects every country on earth – including yours.

In many ways, slavery may look different from the slavery of the Transatlantic slave trade, but modern slavery – as a term – encompasses many forms of slavery, including human trafficking and people being born into slavery.

There are hundreds of definitions of modern slavery. All of these include aspects of control, involuntary actions, and exploitation.

At Anti-Slavery International, we define modern slavery as when an individual is exploited by others, for personal or commercial gain. Whether tricked, coerced, or forced, they lose their freedom. This includes but is not limited to human trafficking, forced labour, and debt bondage.

Our mission is to stop slavery – to secure freedom for everyone, everywhere, always.

Modern slavery is all around us, often hidden in plain sight. People can become enslaved making our clothes, serving our food, picking our crops, working in factories, or working in houses as cooks, cleaners, or nannies. Victims of modern slavery might face violence or threats, be forced into inescapable debt, or have their passport taken away and face being threatened with deportation.

Many people have fallen into this trap because they were trying to escape poverty or insecurity, improve their lives, and support their families. Now, they can't leave.

According to the latest *Global Estimates of Modern Slavery* (2022) from Walk Free, the International Labour Organization, and the International Organization for Migration (IOM):

- 49.6 million people live in modern slavery – in forced labour and forced marriage.
- Roughly a quarter of all victims of modern slavery are children.
- 22 million people are in forced marriages. Two out of five of these people were children.
- Of the 27.6 million people trapped in forced labour, 17.3 million are in forced labour exploitation in the private economy, 6.3 million are in commercial sexual exploitation, and nearly 4 million are in forced labour imposed by state authorities.
- The Covid-19 pandemic has exacerbated the conditions that lead to modern slavery.
- Migrant workers are particularly vulnerable to forced labour.[1]

Types of slavery today

Modern slavery takes many forms. The most common are:

- **Human trafficking:** The use of violence, threats, or coercion to transport, recruit, or harbour people in order to exploit them for purposes such as forced prostitution, labour, criminality, marriage, or organ removal.
- **Forced labour:** Any work or services people are forced to do against their will, usually under threat of punishment.
- **Debt bondage/bonded labour:** The world's most widespread form of slavery. People trapped in poverty

borrow money and are forced to work to pay off the debt, losing control over both their employment conditions and the debt.

- **Descent-based slavery (where people are born into slavery):** A very old form of slavery, where people are treated as property, and their 'slave' status has been passed down the maternal line.
- **Child slavery:** When a child is exploited for someone else's gain. This can include child trafficking, child soldiers, child marriage and child domestic slavery.
- **Forced and early marriage:** When someone is married against their will and cannot leave. Most child marriages can be considered slavery.
- **Domestic servitude:** Domestic work and domestic servitude are not always slavery, and when properly regulated can be an important source of income for many people. However, when someone is working in another person's home, they may be particularly vulnerable to abuses, exploitation, and slavery, as they might be hidden from sight and lack legal protection.

Why are people in slavery today?

People may end up trapped in slavery because they're vulnerable to being tricked, trapped, and exploited, often as a result of poverty and exclusion and because laws do not properly protect them.

Key Facts

- 49.6 million people live in modern slavery – in forced labour and forced marriage.
- 22 million people are in forced marriages. Two out of five of these people were children.

People can be particularly vulnerable to modern slavery when external circumstances push them into taking risky decisions in search of opportunities to provide for their families, or when people find they are simply pushed into jobs in exploitative conditions. Anyone could be pressed into forced labour, but people in vulnerable situations – such as being in debt, or not having access to their passport – are most at risk. Crises like the COVID-19 pandemic and climate change can make people even more vulnerable to exploitation.

Where do we find slavery?

People are being exploited and pushed into slavery all around the world. While it may take different forms, we're committed to ending slavery for everyone, everywhere.

Slavery is a problem in the UK, where many people experience human trafficking, bonded labour, and forced labour. Many products on our local shop shelves might have been made by people in forced labour, but the complex supply chains that businesses have created might make it harder for business to spot exploitation and abuses in their supply chains. In many cases they even hide behind this complexity to evade responsibility. That's why we are pushing for new laws to protect workers and hold businesses accountable for exploitation occurring in their supply chains.

Slavery may be hidden but it exists and it's controlling the lives of millions of people.

[1] Source: Global Estimates of Modern Slavery: Forced Labour and Forced Marriage, Geneva, September 2022

Brainstorm

Can you think of different types of modern slavery?

Research

Can you find any recent stories in the news of modern slavery?

The above information is reprinted with kind permission from Anti-Slavery International.
© 2024 Anti-Slavery International

www.antislavery.org

Modern slavery is increasing – one in every 150 people are victims

By Stephen Hall

- Almost 50 million people, or one in every 150 worldwide, are in situations of modern slavery, according to the International Labour Organization.
- Migrant workers are more than three times more likely to be in forced labour than non-migrant adult workers.
- There were also 22 million people living in situations of forced marriage on any given day in 2021.

Centuries on from the abolition of slavery in major economies worldwide, enforced labour is still a huge problem.

A new International Labour Organization (ILO) report shows that 50 million people – that's one in every 150 worldwide – are in situations of slavery globally. More than 3.3 million of these are children.

The ILO and human rights organisation Walk Free gathered data for the report from nationally representative household surveys. They also collated information from anonymised counter-trafficking data collected by the International Organization for Migration (IOM) and its partners.

Modern slavery is increasing

The UN has set out a goal to end forced child labour by 2025 and abolish all slavery by 2030, but a lot of work still needs to be done to achieve these aims.

The number of people in slavery increased by 2.7 million between 2016 and 2021, according to the ILO, which says this growth has accelerated since the onset of COVID-19. The private economy is the main source of the rise, while state-enforced labour counts for one in seven cases of modern slavery, the report adds.

An increase in extreme poverty since the pandemic began has contributed to the rise in modern slavery, the report

There are almost 50 million people in modern slavery

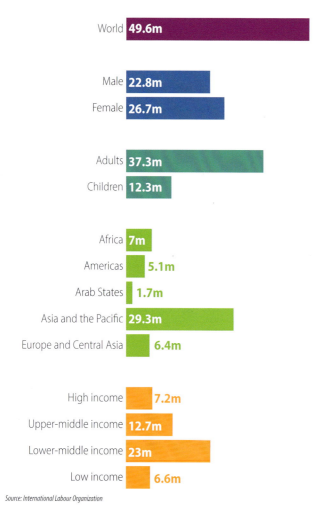

Number of people (millions) in modern slavery, by sex, age, region, and income grouping, 2021

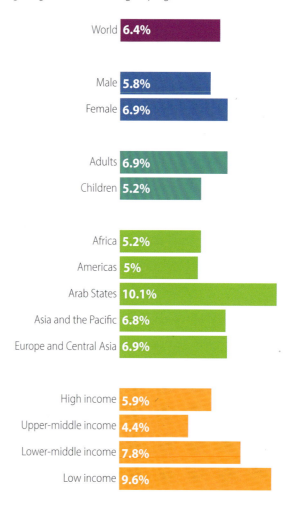

Prevalence (per thousand population) of modern slavery, by sex, age, region, and income grouping, 2021

Source: International Labour Organization

says. The World Bank says that extreme poverty is a major factor driving forced labour.

COVID-19 led to escalated individual debt, resulting in more people being vulnerable to exploitation, the ILO adds.

The sectors driving slavery

Five sectors account for almost 90% of adult forced labour, according to the ILO. These are services (excluding domestic work), manufacturing, construction, agriculture (excluding fishing), and domestic work.

Women in forced labour are far more likely than men to be in domestic work, while men are much more likely to be put to work in the construction sector, the report says.

The private economy is the main source of the rise in modern slavery.

Around 22 million people were in forced marriages in 2021 – an increase of 6.6 million increase from 2016, the ILO says. Over two-thirds of those forced to marry are female. This equates to an estimated 14.9 million women and girls.

Migrants and human trafficking

Migrant adult workers are also more than three times more likely to be in forced labour than non-migrant adult workers, the report says. This is due to an increased risk of unfair or unethical recruitment policies, or irregular or poorly governed migration.

As events such as climate change lead to increased migration worldwide, measures must be taken to protect the displaced from further exploitation.

'Reducing the vulnerability of migrants to forced labour and trafficking in persons depends first and foremost on national policy and legal frameworks that respect, protect, and fulfil the human rights and fundamental freedoms of all migrants – and potential migrants – at all stages of the migration process, regardless of their migration status,' says IOM Director-General António Vitorino.

'The whole of society must work together to reverse these shocking trends, including through implementation of the Global Compact for Migration,' he adds.

How to end modern slavery

To end modern slavery, institutions will need to work collaboratively. 'An all-hands-on-deck approach is needed,' says ILO Director-General Guy Ryder. 'Trade unions, employers' organisations, civil society, and ordinary people all have critical roles to play.'

The ILO report highlights significant actions institutions can take, including:

The private economy is the main source of the rise in modern slavery

The rise in forced labour between 2016 and 2021 was driven entirely by privately-imposed forced labour.

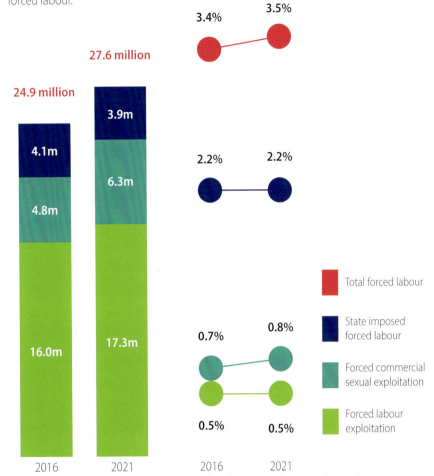

Number and prevalence of people in forced labour, by sub category, 2016 and 2021
Source: International Labour Organization

- Improving and enforcing laws and labour inspections.
- Ending state-imposed forced labour.
- Creating stronger measures to combat forced labour and trafficking in business and supply chains.
- Extending social protection.
- Strengthening legal protections, including raising the legal age of marriage to 18 without exception.

The ILO also highlights the need to address the increased risk of trafficking and forced labour for migrant workers. It calls for the promotion of fair and ethical recruitment, and greater support for women, girls, and vulnerable individuals.

16 September 2022

The above information is reprinted with kind permission from the World Economic Forum.
© 2024 World Economic Forum

www.weforum.org

Modern slavery in United Kingdom

This article is written by Walk Free, the original article and further information on modern slavery can be found at www.Walkfree.org/global-slavery-index

United Kingdom

Estimated number living in modern slavery:
122,000 (1.8 per thousand)

Vulnerability:
14/100

Government response rating:
68/100

Population:
67,886,000

GDP per capita (PPP):
46,527 (current international $)

As a country with relatively high levels of wealth, and therefore more resources to dedicate to addressing modern slavery, the UK has been at the forefront of international efforts to tackle modern slavery and has shown the strongest government response globally. Previously, this reflected strong efforts to coordinate the national response, including by allocating additional funding to anti-slavery efforts domestically and overseas, address underlying risk factors, and strengthen measures to address modern slavery in government and business supply chains. However, in recent years and, in particular, post-Brexit, changes to UK immigration policy have threatened to discriminate against and criminalise vulnerable people, increasing the potential for modern slavery. Modern slavery remains prevalent in the UK, while gaps include lack of protections for vulnerable groups such as migrant workers, and the absence of a National Action Plan or strategy.

Prevalence

The 2023 Global Slavery Index estimates that on any given day in 2021, there were 122,000 people living in modern slavery in the UK. This equates to a prevalence of 1.8 people for every thousand people in the country, and places the UK among the countries with the lowest prevalence of modern slavery in the region (38 out of 47) and globally (145 out of 160). This estimate does not include figures on organ trafficking, which evidence indicates does occur in the UK. In 2022, almost 17,000 potential victims of modern slavery were referred to the UK's National Referral Mechanism (NRM), representing a 33% increase on the previous year and the highest number of referrals since the NRM began in 2009. The UK government links this increase to a rise in the number of detections by regulatory first responders at the British border. Despite the rise in referrals, modern slavery likely remains heavily underreported given our prevalence data. Official modern slavery statistics in the UK highlight a gendered aspect, with 78% of all individuals referred to the NRM in 2022 being male. In 2022, for the first time, Albanian nationals overtook UK nationals as the most commonly referred nationality, with Eritrean nationals being third.

Forced labour

Forced labour exploitation

Potential victims were most commonly referred to the NRM for labour exploitation in 2022, accounting for 30% (2,141) of potential referrals. In the same year, more than 7,300 calls for help were received by the UK Modern Slavery helpline, run by Unseen, with an increase of 134% in cases of labour exploitation in comparison to previous years. Forced labour is reported in many sectors including farming, hospitality, beauty, construction, manufacturing, car washes, domestic service and other service industries. Many of these industries rely heavily on migrant workers. Recent evidence shows exploitation of migrant workers within the government's seasonal worker visa scheme, which has rapidly expanded from 2,500 visas issued in its 2019 pilot, to 47,000 in 2023. For example, in 2022, investigations revealed cases involving the exploitation of Nepali and Indonesian migrant workers, who were made to pay extortionate fees to agents working for UK licenced recruitment companies to secure jobs on fruit farms under the scheme. The Gangmasters and Labour Abuse Authority (GLAA) concluded a subsequent investigation in 2023 resulting in a Nepali agency losing its licence and a Slavery and Trafficking Risk Order handed to the two company directors.

Domestic workers, who are often migrant workers, are also particularly vulnerable to modern slavery; a recent investigation found that domestic workers – predominantly women from the Philippines and Indonesia – are held in domestic servitude in the households of London-based diplomats. According to the investigation, at least 13 migrant domestic workers employed by diplomats were referred through the NRM between 2017 and 2021, after experiencing passport retention, wage withholding, food deprivation, and confinement to the household, among other abuses.

Forced criminal activity is a prevalent form of forced labour across the UK, including forced begging, forced theft, forced work on cannabis farms, and financial abuse and fraud. Children are particularly vulnerable, with the latest government statistics showing that 41% of all NRM referrals were for children, with forced criminality being the most common type of exploitation. Since 2020, there has been a sharp increase in the identification of children in 'county lines' cases – a term used to describe the recruitment of children by gangs for the purpose of transporting illegal drugs across the country. In 2022, over 2,200 county lines referrals were flagged, accounting for 13% of all referrals received in that year. The majority (75%) of these referrals were for boys.

Forced commercial sexual exploitation of adults

14% of all referrals made in 2022 were cases of sexual exploitation. The NRM experienced a 130% rise in Albanian females being referred to the service, which is largely resulting from reports of sexual exploitation.

The Salvation Army delivers the UK government's primary contract to manage support services for survivors of modern slavery in England and Wales. Their latest statistics show that

issues: Human Rights   30   Chapter 2: Human Rights Today sexual exploitation was the second most common referral, particularly among those of Nigerian, Iranian, and Albanian nationality. While females remain the most impacted (88% of referrals), the number of men identified by the service as having experienced sexual exploitation had nearly tripled compared to the last reporting period. UK nationals also experience forced commercial sexual exploitation in the UK.

Commercial sexual exploitation of children

Commercial sexual exploitation referrals made under the NRM among girls alone rose by 26% in 2022 to 331, and represented the most common form of referral for these individuals. Analysis of police-recorded crime data in England and Wales in 2021/2022 reveals there were 17,486 crimes logged by police where children had been sexually exploited – an average of 48 offences a day. This is an increase of 10% compared to the preceding year, with the majority being female referrals. This includes children who were trafficked after being threatened with violence or the promise of a better life. Recent police data analysis also highlights a surge in child abuse image offences, with an increase of almost 66% on figures from five years ago. There are reports that organised criminal groups across the UK use social media to produce and share child sexual abuse materials, which may amount to modern slavery.

Forced marriage

Forced marriage remains hidden in the UK and ascertaining the number of victims is a challenge. The national Forced Marriage Unit (FMU) reported that it responded to 337 forced marriage referrals in 2021, compared to 759 cases in 2020. The significant reduction in referrals was primarily attributed to the impacts of the COVID-19 pandemic, as well as a procedural change that saw more cases (868 total) being categorised as 'general enquiries.' For general enquiries the FMU may be required to give general advice, rather than 'advice and support' cases, where an individual is deemed at risk of, or affected by, forced marriage. Of advice and support cases, the majority of individuals (72%) were in the UK at the time of referral, with 76% being British or dual nationality, compared to 19% who were non-British nationals. Of identified cases, 22% were under the age of 15, and 13% were 16–17 years of age. In 2018, in the first successful prosecution of its kind, a British woman was found guilty of deceiving her teenage daughter into travelling to Pakistan for a forced marriage.

Organ trafficking

While official statistics regarding organ trafficking are unavailable, organ trafficking does occur in the UK. In 2022, Ike Ekweremadi, a Nigerian politician and his wife, were convicted under the Modern Slavery Act for organ trafficking – the first conviction of its kind. The couple brought a man from Lagos to the UK to become an organ donor for the couple's daughter in exchange for £7,000 (US$8,700) and the promise of establishing a life in the UK.

Imported products at risk of modern slavery

The UK is not only affected by modern slavery within its borders: as one of the world's largest economies, the UK – like other G20 countries – is exposed to the risk of modern slavery through the products it imports. Nearly two-thirds of all forced labour cases are linked to global supply chains, with workers exploited across a wide range of sectors and at

Table 1: Imports of products at risk of modern slavery to the United Kingdom

Product at risk of modern slavery	Import value (in billions of US$)	Source countries
Garments	10.1	Argentina, Bangladesh, Brazil, China, India, Malaysia, Vietnam
Electronics	14.7	China, Malaysia
Fish	0.3	China, Ghana, Indonesia, Thailand, Taiwan
Textiles	0.5	China
Timber	0.5	Russia, Brazil, Peru

Source: Walk Free

every stage of the supply chain. Most forced labour occurs in the lowest tiers of supply chains; that is, in the extraction of raw materials and in production stages. Given the G20's level of influence in the global economy, it is critical to examine their imports at risk of forced labour and efforts to address this risk. The UK imports US$26.1 billion products at-risk of being made using forced labour annually. Table 1 below highlights the top five most valuable products (according to US$ value per annum) imported by the UK that are at risk of being produced under conditions of modern slavery.

Vulnerability

Governance issues	12/100
Lack of basic needs	25/100
Inequality	28/100
Disenfranchised groups	30/100
Effects of conflict	34/100
Overall weighted average	14/100

Source: Walk Free

The UK is among the least vulnerable countries to modern slavery in the Europe and Central Asia region, however several factors drive the risk of modern slavery, including discrimination of migrants and those fleeing conflict and other crises, increasing costs of living, and marginalisation of minority groups.

Discriminatory attitudes towards migrants, asylum seekers, and refugees are the strongest drivers of vulnerability, which manifest in a hostile environment for those arriving and living in the UK. The risks facing temporary migrant workers

issues: Human Rights   31   Chapter 2: Human Rights Today

typically result from deception or fees incurred throughout the migration process and limited oversight, monitoring, and enforcement of worker rights and conditions in industries with high numbers of temporary migrant workers. Recruitment and migration fees can leave migrant workers in thousands of pounds worth of debt before entering the UK, which is then exploited by managers and gangmasters. While such gangmasters often provide a minimum wage in order to create the appearance of compliance with UK legislation, it is commonplace to deduct pay for the purposes of clothing, accommodation, transportation, or training, leaving vulnerable workers in a cycle of debt.

Refugees and those seeking asylum are also at heightened risk of exploitation in the UK, due to social and cultural isolation, and a lack of access to basic resources and employment opportunities, often compounded by an insecure immigration status. Ukrainian citizens who came to the UK under the government's flagship Homes for Ukraine scheme are vulnerable to exploitation. An Office for National Statistics survey found that many are struggling to find work, access education, and find rented accommodation. Concerningly, 40% of people surveyed also indicated that they would not know how to report exploitation.

Growing inequality, poverty and lack of access to basic needs drives vulnerability to modern slavery. The cost-of-living crisis in the UK will likely make more people vulnerable to exploitation. In the year 2022, 2.1 million people, or 3% of families, used a food bank. Evidence shows that lack of support from authorities on housing, economic situation, mental health or education creates a vacuum that can leave children vulnerable to criminal gangs and exploitation in county lines. Children who are in care, or who go missing from home or care facilities, are more vulnerable to trafficking and exploitation. ECPAT UK (Every Child Protected Against Trafficking) found that one in three trafficked children in the UK in 2020 went missing from local authority care, which was a rise of 25% since the last statistics in 2018. Such children tend to be more susceptible to the attention given by traffickers who groom the children through giving of gifts or attention, and then introduce them to drugs and alcohol before subjecting them to sexual violence or forced criminality. Child asylum seekers have also gone missing from hotels, targeted by organised crime groups, and forced to work or sell drugs.

Government response

Survivors identified and supported	73/100
Criminal justice mechanisms	77/100
National and regional level coordination	75/100
Risk factors are addressed	79/100
Government and business supply chains	38/100
Total	72/100

Overall, the UK had the strongest government response to modern slavery, both in the region and globally. This reflects some strong efforts to address risk factors, establish criminal justice mechanisms, and tackle forced labour in supply chains. However, significant gaps remain, including the need to strengthen measures to support survivors, while recent and proposed changes to UK immigration policy have increased vulnerability.

The UK had among the strongest criminal justice mechanisms in the region and criminalises most forms of modern slavery in line with international conventions under the 2015 Modern Slavery Act and the Anti-Social Behaviour, Crime and Policing Act 2014. The UK also raised the legal age of marriage to 18, without exception, under the Marriage and Civil Partnership (Minimum Age) Act 2022 in February 2023. However, gaps in the criminal justice response remain. The government has not ratified the ILO Domestic Workers Convention, 2011, despite the significant risks that domestic workers face. Additionally, the law does not fully recognise that victims should not be treated as criminals for conduct that occurred while under the control of criminals. Although s45 of the Modern Slavery Act provides some protection from criminalisation, it is narrow in application as it does not apply to all crimes. This is concerning given the number of individuals, including children, who experience forced criminality. The UK's previous Independent Anti-Slavery Commissioner highlighted that current legal protections were inadequate to protect victims of modern slavery from criminalisation, and that police often did not consider the possibility of forced criminality at the beginning of an investigation. Further, the European Court of Human Rights ruled in 2021 that the UK failed to protect two victims of trafficking who had been forced to work on cannabis farms, by arresting and charging them with drugs-related offences.

The UK's modern slavery strategy was last released in 2014. The government committed to review this strategy and publish an updated version in 2022, however at the time of writing no new strategy has been published. At the time of writing, there has been no announcement of the new Independent Anti-Slavery Commissioner since Dame Sara Thornton stepped down in April 2022, raising concerns that there is nobody holding the government accountable for a robust response to modern slavery. The Home Office continued funding the Modern Slavery and Organised Immigration Crime Programme with an additional £1.4 million (US$1.75 million) to support the police in their response efforts. An independent review of the government's overseas spending on modern slavery programming found the £200 million (US$250 million) programme had been successful at raising global awareness of modern slavery, that programmes were mostly on track to meet their targets, and cross-government collaboration had been strong. However, the Independent Commission for Aid Impact review also found there was limited evidence of longer-term impact, survivors were not effectively consulted, and that there was limited overall evidence of effective measures to tackle modern slavery. The Department of Justice in Northern Ireland established a Modern Slavery and Human Trafficking Branch in 2021, which was tasked with formulating the government's strategy to combat modern slavery and human trafficking. In January 2022, Scotland released its fourth annual progress report on the Trafficking and Exploitation Strategy, which was developed in consultation with survivors.

Since 2018, the government has taken steps to tackle forced labour in supply chains, but has fallen short of implementing the full suite of commitments it made in 2020 in response to a consultation on the transparency in supply chains provisions under the Modern Slavery Act. The government had committed to mandate the areas statements produced under Section 54 of the Modern Slavery Act must cover, publish new guidance, oblige companies to submit statements to a centralised registry, establish a single reporting deadline, and extend the Act's application to public sector bodies. The government did publish guidance for tackling modern slavery in government supply chains and released the first government modern slavery statement in 2020. In a move to enhance transparency, the government also launched a central registry in 2021 for statements produced under the Act and required ministerial departments to annually produce individual modern slavery statements. However, the remaining commitments are yet to be implemented, while submitting statements to the registry remains voluntary. Many countries across the European Union have implemented mandatory human rights due diligence legislation (mHRDD), while the EU is considering a Directive on Corporate Sustainability Due Diligence (CSDD), which would surpass any reforms to Section 54 of the Modern Slavery Act.

The government has developed alternative measures to tackle forced labour. In a landmark amendment to the Health and Care Act (Article 81), the government implemented regulations to ban the National Health Service from importing goods or services tainted by modern slavery and set out steps to be taken to assess the level of risk associated with individual suppliers. The Procurement Bill has similar regulations. The government also established a global human rights sanction regime in 2020, using powers under the Sanctions and Anti-Money Laundering Act 2018. These sanctions have also been used against those committing forced labour and forced marriage.

Despite these positive steps, a number of actions undermine the government's response to modern slavery. Since Brexit, the government has made or proposed changes to policy that infringe upon or jeopardise human rights. In June 2022, the Bill of Rights Bill was introduced to Parliament as a replacement for the Human Rights Act, 1998, which incorporates and makes the rights contained in the European Convention on Human Rights (ECHR) domestically enforceable. There are numerous concerns over how the Bill of Rights would change or remove existing provisions, including introducing additional barriers to justice for victims of modern slavery via court procedures, and imposing higher thresholds for challenges to deportations, and reports have since indicated that the Bill has been halted. Similarly, the UK's shift towards a more hostile and discriminatory environment towards migration has made it increasingly difficult for vulnerable people including modern slavery victims to access essential support and services.

Most recently, in March 2023, the government proposed the Illegal Immigration Bill, which aims to detain and swiftly remove anyone entering the country 'illegally' in response to individuals arriving by boat across the English Channel. The Bill contravenes multiple human rights conventions that the government has ratified and will prevent modern slavery victims from reaching safety and accessing support. In the absence of alternative avenues to reach the UK and in some cases reunite with family, asylum seekers are risking their lives and traversing the English Channel in often overloaded and unseaworthy boats. The increasing curtailment of clear and accessible pathways to safe and legal migration pose a serious threat to the safety of vulnerable people and exposes them to the risk of modern slavery.

Severe labour shortages after Brexit and COVID-19 have increased reliance on migrant workers, but despite this, the UK government has failed to effectively respond to the heightened vulnerability of migrant and seasonal workers, with some policies amplifying their modern slavery risks. The government has committed to establishing a single enforcement body for employment rights to better protect vulnerable workers and ensure a level playing field for the majority of employers complying with the law, but the body has yet to be established. As part of a review of visas to tackle labour shortages, the quota for seasonal worker visas for horticulture in the UK has risen to 47,000, an increase of 17,000 compared to 2022 figures, with the potential for a further 10,000 visas should the demand be proven. While this would be a positive step if decent working conditions could be guaranteed, the rise coincides with a budget cuts to the national GLAA, with inspections of current labour providers at an all-time low. Further, without guaranteed work/ income over the six-month period, workers may become unable to repay migration costs and face associated exploitation risks. There is urgent need for an increase in regulation and enforcement of the scheme, to avoid further risks of labour exploitation.

In a similar step to plug national labour shortages, the UK and Nepali governments announced an agreement in August 2022 to increase the recruitment of Nepalese health workers in the UK. Although the Department of Health has hailed the scheme as ethical and regulated, critics have raised concerns about the notorious mistreatment from Nepali recruitment agencies, often unable to be properly regulated by the UK, and the high potential for worker exploitation. The UK Overseas Domestic Worker Visa has been criticised for creating exploitation risks. This visa allows migrant workers to enter the UK for up to six months to work as domestic workers in private households, but effectively ties them to their employer for their right to remain in the UK. The visa remains in force despite evidence of its links to worker exploitation and calls for reform from civil society and survivor groups.

The above information is reprinted with kind permission from Walk Free.

This article is written by Walk Free, the original article and further information on modern slavery can be found at Walkfree.org/global-slavery-index

© 2024 Minderoo Foundation Pty Ltd

www.walkfree.org

issues: Human Rights   Chapter 2: Human Rights Today

Ten ways that Saudi Arabia violates human rights

Saudi Arabia makes headlines hosting glittering events, securing famous footballers including Cristiano Ronaldo to play in its national league, and for innventive ideas such as the notorious 'The Line' city concept.

But the reality for people living in Saudi Arabia, is one where their basic human rights are ignored, their freedoms are restricted, and punishment is severe.

For example, blogger Raif Badawi was sentenced to 1,000 lashes and ten years in prison for 'insulting Islam' and founding an online forum for political debate. He was due to be flogged 50 times every week. In 2022, Raif was finally released, but he faces a travel ban, meaning that after not seeing his family for 12 years, he will have to wait another nine years.

Raif's case is just the tip of the iceberg for the Gulf Kingdom's appalling human rights record.

Here are 10 ways Saudi Arabia is violating its citizens' human rights:

1. Executions are on the increase

Saudi Arabia executed 196 people in 2022. On 12th March, the authorities killed 81 men in one day – the single largest mass execution in recent decades. The country ranks as the second highest for use of the death penalty.

2. Women are widely discriminated against

Women and girls remain subject to discrimination in law and in practice. The male guardianship system was enshrined into law in 2022, and means that women must have a male legal guardian – and they cannot choose who this is.

Also, many women, such as Loujain, who supported a campaign against a ban on women drivers were imprisoned and harassed, despite the fact that the law was then changed to allow women to drive.

3. Many are tortured while detained

In 2022, Saudi Arabian authorities arbitrarily detained Ethiopian men, women, and children for up to 18 months in inhumane conditions and tortured and otherwise ill-treated them before forcibly returning them to Ethiopia. They were held in overcrowded cells with inadequate access to food, water, sanitation, and healthcare in two detention centres prior to their deportation. At least 12 men died.

4. Migrant workers treated poorly

According to the Interior Ministry, there is a consistent crackdown on foreign nationals, with 479,000 being returned to their home country out of 678,000 arrested. During that same period, 14,511 foreign nationals, most of them Ethiopians and Yemenis, where violence has forced many to flee, were arrested for crossing the border irregularly from Yemen into Saudi Arabia.

5. Crackdown on free media and press

The Saudi authorities control domestic media and journalists can be imprisoned for a variety of 'crimes'.

Saudi authorities including the Crown Prince sanctioned the brutal murder the journalist Jamal Khashoggi after he had been critical of the government. Leadership in the country has never been held to account for their role.

6. No free speech

Besides Raif Badawi, dozens more outspoken activists remain behind bars, simply for exercising their rights to freedom of expression, association, and assembly.

Many of Saudi Arabia's prominent and independent human rights defenders have been imprisoned, threatened into silence, or fled the country.

7. Unfair trials

Trials against people are often grossly unfair and courts impose long prison sentences. People are often held in solitary confinement without any communication.

Salma al-Shehab, a student of Leeds University and mother of two, was sentenced to 27 years in prison on terrorism-related offences after a grossly unfair trial for publishing tweets in support of women's rights.

8. Travel bans

Many human rights activists who have been released from unfair imprisonment, face continued punishment. Many are given travel bans, meaning they are unable to leave the country and see loved ones.

9. Forced evictions

Over half a million people in the city of Jeddah have been forcibly evicted and their homes demolished, to make way for luxury hotels and buildings.

A compensation scheme, announced after the demolitions, excludes foreign nationals, who make up nearly half of those impacted.

10. No protests

Protests and demonstrations are illegal. Those who defy the ban face arrest, prosecution and imprisonment on charges such as 'inciting people against the authorities'.

So, the next time you see a headline about Saudi Arabia hosting the men's World Cup, taking over a UK football club or releasing outlandish ideas for our cities, keep in mind how the country's authorities treat its own people.

Saudi Arabia isn't the only country that is repressing the right to protest, even in the UK, the government is cracking down this fundamental right.

12 January 2024

The above information is reprinted with kind permission from Amnesty International UK.

© Amnesty International UK 2024

www.amnesty.org.uk

issues: Human Rights   34   Chapter 2: Human Rights Today

The silent chains of Saudi Arabia: my fight for my daughter and our freedom

By Bethany Alhaidari, Human Rights Foundation (HRF) Senior Fellow on Human Trafficking

In 2011, while working in Tunisia, my life completely changed. I witnessed the start of the Arab Spring and fall of Tunisia's dictator, Zine el-Abidine Ben Ali, due to a popular uprising against injustice. As an American citizen, it was the first time I truly understood how vital freedom, human rights, dignity, and democratic principles were.

I switched my life path and entered academia, conducting graduate human rights and socio-legal research on one of the world's most notorious human rights violators and dictatorships: Saudi Arabia. I embarked on a journey to research, write, learn, and experience. Along the way, I met some of the most inspiring Saudi human rights defenders, several of whom ended up in jail. I married a Saudi activist who was supportive of my work at the time, gave birth to my beautiful daughter Zaina, and started a business.

While my journey started with the pursuit of knowledge and understanding, I eventually experienced firsthand the exact human rights violations I was researching.

My marriage took a turn for the worse. Gathering the courage to seek freedom from an abusive relationship introduced the harsh realities of male guardianship, the kafala system, and the status of women under the country's law. Being female and foreign, Saudi Arabia's systems placed a heavy burden on me – a weight I wasn't prepared to face in Saudi Arabian courts.

In a society where women are bound by the decisions of their male guardians and where a woman's word is not equal to a man's under the law, my voice was suddenly silenced, and the interests of my daughter were completely ignored. Basic freedoms I had once taken for granted – using my bank account or accessing money, legal representation, seeking medical care, travelling without risking deportation, and running my business – were stripped away. In their child custody assessments, the Saudi court viewed my culture and traditions as more problematic than abuse and neglect. My attempts to seek safety were met with injustice, abuse, and humiliation; I was ultimately forced to go back into the arms of my abuser.

The reality is that many women, including foreigners like me, still grapple with the chains of the kafala and male guardianship systems. Women are subjected to discrimination, it increases if they are not a Saudi citizen and especially from a developing country. More rights are stripped away for not supporting the government, or converting to the regime's highly politicized interpretation of Islam.

On 15 December 2019, after two years of entrapment, wrongful detention, a 10-year travel ban, criminal charges on false allegations, my parental rights being taken away, and then being forced to degradingly return to my abuser,

my daughter and I managed to escape Saudi Arabia. I held my breath in anticipation on our journey from Riyadh to Seattle. I watched the clouds clear as our flight was landing to reveal the Space Needle, an icon of the city where I was born and now a symbol of my freedom and dignity. After years of being terrified, deprived of dignity and protection, we were finally safe.

There was one looming threat: a Saudi court order for our return to Riyadh 28 days after I landed. A Washington State superior court evaluated our case and took jurisdiction on human rights grounds. That ruling has allowed us to remain in the United States for the past four years.

The world is under the false impression that Saudi Arabia has improved and reformed its abhorrent human rights record. This is primarily due to billion-dollar investments by the Saudi regime into top public relations and lobbying firms in the West, while heavily whitewashing to distract from their human rights violations. This misinformation has cost me tens of thousands of dollars and countless hours in courtrooms trying to dispel it over the years, and threatens my daughter's security and safety.

Now, everything is on the line again. The ruling that allows my daughter to remain in the United States has been appealed.

On 24 October my legal team at Perkins Coie will stand in front of a three-judge appellate panel and again plead for our lives. If I lose, my daughter will be forced to return to Saudi Arabia. My daughter would not be able to return to the US without her father's permission until she is at least 21. I would have no legal recourse or right to see her in Saudi Arabia.

I could not follow her without risking my life. In March 2021, I was accused of being a spy in a video produced by Saudi media outlets, a crime that has historically resulted in punishment by public beheading. These allegations led to threats against my colleagues and friends in Saudi Arabia, and to Saudi lawyers being forced to rescind their representation of me.

I gave up everything to save and protect my daughter and myself in 2019. It is difficult to face the current reality; to think that such an injustice could ever occur, especially in my home state of Washington.

What we need now is a genuine commitment from global leaders, legislators, and human rights organisations to advocate for the rights of women and children in Saudi Arabia. We must ensure that no mother has to face the heart-wrenching decision of leaving their child behind, and no child is deprived of the love and care they rightfully deserve. This will not be possible until the male guardianship system and the kafala systems are abolished. Countless women and children remain trapped by these systems. I'm urging world leaders to recognise and address the discrepancies between rhetoric and reality when it comes to human rights in Saudi Arabia.

In my heart, I remain hopeful for a just outcome in our case, where truth prevails, and the complex contradictions and violations in the Saudi Arabian legal system will be clear. I refuse to believe that we could be returned to a legal nightmare where we are treated as little more than the property of a man.

My daughter is currently free and safe in the only home she knows with the only caretaker she knows. She can grow up to participate in her government. She can be a judge or a senator. She can choose who she wants to marry. She can choose her religion. She can be a human rights activist, criticise her government, or embrace being queer without having to risk her life.

All of this could be taken away in Washington state on 24 October if she is forced to return to Saudi Arabia. There isn't a way to prepare when so much is on the line. Regardless of the outcome, I will continue to fight for my daughter's freedom and basic rights and for every mother who wishes for nothing more than a safe, free, and loving environment for their child.

24 October 2023

The above information is reprinted with kind permission from Human Rights Foundation.
© 2024 Human Rights Foundation

www.hrf.org

12 women activists and leaders making the world a better place

From championing refugee rights to rescuing their children from destroyed homes, we're celebrating these brave women who won't wait for change to happen.

When a crisis hits, it's women and girls that are most affected. They experience increased gender-based violence and a loss of income can put them more at risk of early, child, or forced marriage. But instead of waiting for conflicts to end, for someone else to step in, or for laws to pass to help them, women are stepping up and being the first responders, changemakers, and activists that their families, local communities, and women across the world need.

In honour of International Women's Day, here are 12 women who are making the world a safer, better place, for everyone.

Malala Yousafzai

Malala was 15-years-old when she was targeted for advocating for girls' right to education in Pakistan. A gunman tried to kill her as she walked home from school. Malala survived the attack and she and her family moved to the UK, where she launched the Malala Fund, a non-profit organisation that advocates for girls' education.

With more than 130 million girls out of school today, Malala continues to fight for girls' right to learn.

In 2014, at the age of 17, she became the youngest Nobel Peace Prize laureate for her work and the United Nations launched the 'Malala Day,' in honour of the young Pakistani activist's fight for universal education.

Sara Mardini

Sara is a Syrian former competition swimmer, lifeguard, and human rights activist, who took part in search and rescue missions, saving refugees making the crossing from Turkey to Greece.

Sara and her younger sister, now Olympic swimmer Yusra Mardini, fled from Syria in 2015. When the boat they were escaping on started to sink in the Aegean Sea, the sisters swam the boat to safety, a journey chronicled in the Netflix movie, *The Swimmers*.

> 'I talk them through it… I tell them, 'I know what you feel, because I've been through it. I lived it, and I survived', and they feel better, because I am a refugee just like them.'

After the sisters were granted political asylum in Germany, Sara joined a non-governmental organisation that helped refugees arriving on the Greek island of Lesbos, working as a translator. 'I talk them through it,' Sara said. I tell them, 'I know what you feel, because I've been through it. I lived it, and I survived', and they feel better, because I am a refugee just like them.'

Sara's involvement in Lesbos led to her and other human rights activists being arrested in 2018, with charges which have been refuted heavily by organisations like Amnesty International. In January 2023, Sara went on trial with 24 other humanitarian aid workers, facing up to 25 years in prison for charges of 'espionage,' 'migrant smuggling,' and 'money laundering' in Greece. After the court ruled that the charges of espionage were partially inadmissible, Sara and the other aid workers await a second trial to determine the charge of 'migrant smuggling.'

Halima Aden

Halima Aden is a Somali-American fashion model and activist. She was born at Kakuma Refugee Camp in Kenya and moved to the United States aged six.

Halima broke boundaries at every step of her career, becoming the first hijab-wearing model to be signed to a major agency, walk international runways, and appear on the cover of *Vogue* magazine. Soon after, Halima became a United Nations Children's Fund (UNICEF) ambassador, through which she advocates for children's rights and uses her platform to raise funds and awareness for the global refugee crisis.

> 'I need to be the person the kids in the refugee camps can relate to. The greatest thing I could give them is hope'.

'I need to be the person the kids in the refugee camps can relate to. The greatest thing I could give them is hope,' Halima says. 'I want everyone to live to their full potential without having to fear someone will try to knock them down or discriminate against them.'

Waad Al-Kateab*

Waad is a Syrian activist who started out as a citizen journalist for Channel 4 News in 2011, through which her reports on the war were broadcast in the UK. Over time, as the war intensified, Waad chose to stay and document her life in Aleppo, during which she met her partner and gave birth to their first daughter, Sama.

For Sama, Waad's debut feature film which was dedicated to her first daughter, swept the awards ceremonies across the globe, winning Best Documentary at the BAFTAs, Cannes Film Festival, and the Emmys.

Having fled Aleppo in 2016, Waad, her husband, and her two daughters, now live in the United Kingdom, where she continues to work as a filmmaker/reporter for Channel 4 News, as well as being a mentor for female journalists. Outside of film, Waad dedicates time to her advocacy campaign, Action for Sama, which was set up to turn the worldwide support for the film into positive action for Syrians.

*Al-Kateab is the chosen pseudonym surname to protect Waad's family.

Nadia Murad

Nadia is an Iraqi Yazidi human rights activist who now lives in Germany. In 2014, Nadia was kidnapped from her home in Iraq by members of the group known as ISIS and held captive for three months.

Following her escape, Nadia became a powerful advocate for women in conflict settings and survivors of sexual violence. This resulted in her being awarded the 2018 Nobel Peace Prize – the first Iraqi and Yazidi to have done so. The same year, she founded Nadia's Initiative, an organisation dedicated to providing advocacy and assistance to victims of genocide.

'I want to be the last girl in the world with a story like mine. We must not only imagine a better future for women, children, and persecuted minorities; we must work consistently to make it happen – prioritising humanity, not war.'

Rima Sultana Rimu

Rima Sultana Rimu, human rights activist, sitting at a table with a pen in her hand

As a member of 'Young Women Leaders for Peace,' Rima Sultana Rimu has been recognised for her outstanding work providing educational resources for women and children in Rohingya refugee camps in her native Bangladesh. Using radio broadcasts and theatre performances as well as more traditional classroom teaching methods, Rimu spreads awareness of the UN Security Council's recommendations on women, peace, and security. She also serves as a resource for members of the Rohingya community facing issues like child marriage and domestic violence.

'I am determined to bring gender equality to Bangladesh. I believe in the power of women and girls to fight for our rights. We will succeed.'

Maryna

Maryna is a mother of two whose home in Ukraine was heavily damaged by missile strikes. On one occasion, Maryna's three-year-old son and 11-year-old daughter were both in the house when a missile struck. With her husband away on a business trip, Maryna was alone with her children in the house. At first, she did not even realise that a missile had hit, and it was only until she heard her young son crying that she realised he was stuck under building fragments. Immediately, Maryna jumped into action and pulled him out.

'My daughter was so surprised…I said, 'I knew I was running out of time. I mean, even if you're covered with something, I'll dig you out, give you to an ambulance, and you'll live on.'

Since then, the International Rescue Committee (IRC) has been helping Maryna register for financial compensation for damages, as well as providing essential items to prepare for the winter ahead.

Zahra

Zahra is an Afghan refugee, journalist and single mum. She and her two children, aged 11 and 10, fled from Afghanistan to the UK in August 2021, forcing her to leave her dream job as a TV news anchor.

In 2022, Zahra took part in the IRC's leadership training, and now advocates for women's rights on a global scale, telling her story of fleeing conflict to the United Nations. Settling into the UK, Zahra has dreams of studying for a Master's degree and restarting her career as a journalist, while being an advocate for women's rights in Afghanistan and all over the world.

'I want the world to stay with Afghanistan and all in the world who are in danger,' Zahra says. 'There shouldn't be any difference between refugees and how people from different countries are treated. I want equality for everyone, whether they're from Ukraine or Afghanistan or anywhere else, they should have the same rights.'

Omaira

'That's the biggest challenge, reaching all women… and teaching them that there is no reason to live with violence or to live with fear every day.'

Omaira is a Women's Protection and Empowerment Advocate from Colombia. A survivor of gender-based violence, her experiences drove her to participate in an IRC-run programme funded by ECHO, as part of a group of 25 women. Through the programme, Omaira was empowered to take ownership for her community and identify ways to prevent, and even respond to, gender-based violence cases that her neighbours might experience. As an advocate within her community, Omaira receives training on how to listen to survivors, as well as how to emotionally take care of herself and protect against the effects of second-hand trauma.

'You, as a survivor, can give a hand to someone who at the moment is a victim,' Omaira says on what she's learnt from being a support worker. 'You have to say "you're no longer a victim, you're going to be a survivor."'

Mokube

Growing up in her community in south-west Cameroon, Mokube experienced discrimination by men who ridiculed her for receiving an education. Whenever she tried to defend herself, many refused to listen.

'They insulted me… They said that I wasn't fulfilling my duties as a woman – that I'm instead wasting my time studying,' Mokube says.

This led Mokube to put herself forward for training to become a community advocate on gender-based violence at a programme run by the IRC, to learn even more about the issue and to help educate the wider community. Now, Mokube helps empower other women and girls in her community to stand up for themselves and take an active part in helping others.

Ala'a
'Never give up, and never let anyone say she's a woman and can't do it.'

Ala'a set up her own vegetable shop during the height of the economic crisis in Lebanon, determined to help get her family out of debt. She received funding support and financial training from the IRC.

Drawing upon years of experience from her father, her shop is now thriving – even through the economic crisis and electricity shortages – and she hopes to expand it into a franchise one day.

Also mother to a five-year old girl called Imane, Ala'a is a fierce believer that women can do it all. She doesn't see her being a business owner and working long hours affecting her ability to be a caring mother who can give her daughter everything she wants.

'You know society's view on women is that women are only housewives and mothers. It's quite the opposite,' Ala'a asserts. 'A woman can do anything, be a vegetable grocer or a mechanic. In my opinion, there's nothing a woman can't do.'

Warsan Shire

Warsan Shire, featured in Beyonce's *Lemonade*, was born in Kenya to Somali refugees and raised in London.

Known to many as 'a compelling voice on black womanhood and the Africa diaspora,' Shire started writing poetry as a teenager. One of her poems, *Home*, became a rallying cry for refugees and those who support them.

She writes:

no one leaves home unless

home is the mouth of a shark

you only run for the border

when you see the whole city running as well.

Shire was honoured as London's first-ever Young Poet Laureate in 2014.

7 March 2023

The above information is reprinted with kind permission from International Rescue Committee.

© International Rescue Committee, 2024

www.rescue.org

Young activists share their vision for human rights

Anghelina, Anna Katherina, Doris and Fran have a common vision for their future and the future of human rights.

For Anna Katherina, a 17-year-old defender from Venezuela, there is no question that human rights are inherent to everyone.

'They are not something you earn or win, they are something you are born with and that everyone should have,' she said. 'Even though we have documents such as the Universal Declaration of Human Rights that state that every human can access those rights, the reality is completely different sometimes.'

Anna Katherina explained that her engagement with human rights stemmed from being a victim of bullying from a young age because of her family's social and economic status – they live in a poor area of her city. Two years ago, she started her activism against bullying to help other children experiencing similar violence.

'[Children] have the capacity to talk about what affects us and challenges our daily lives. It's important that not only people who work on human rights and children's rights advocate for us, but that we are also given the space for us to talk about what happened to us,' she said.

Anna Katherina was speaking on the side lines of the Human Rights 75 high-level event that took place in December 2023 in Geneva to mark the 75th anniversary of the Universal Declaration of Human Rights. She and three other young activists hailing from the four corners of the world came together with UN Human Rights in 2023 through the Children's Advisory Team of the non-governmental organisation Child Rights Connect to promote the Human Rights 75 Initiative, and build the capacity of other children who, like them, wish to engage with world leaders and UN Human Rights in strengthening their human rights.

Her modest origins were also the reason why Doris, a 15-year-old from Zambia, wanted to focus her interests on the economy, education, and human rights. Living in a 'shanty compound' in Kabwe district, north of the capital Lusaka, when the COVID-19 pandemic broke, she realised that she had no other choice but to make her own voice heard to bring change to her community.

Participating in the Human Rights 75 event in Geneva gave her a more direct connection to global decision-makers, 'the people who can actually help us,' Doris said.

'Children do have stories to tell, but they don't have platforms on which they can share their stories,' she added. 'When I first started my advocacy four years ago, I would never see changes. I would return from school, tired, and talk to local leaders about people needing food. They would agree to meet with me but did nothing about the situation.'

'Children's rights are human rights but not all institutions have that perspective. They usually talk about children's rights, but we have no actions,' said Anghelina, a 16-year-old from Moldova.

'Participation in the Human Rights 75 forum was designed for all civil society, institutions, governments, and country representatives to take our voices on global issues into consideration and allow us to participate in decision-making processes regarding our own rights and global issues.'

Anghelina started her human rights defender journey at 14, spurred by her own experiences of injustices and human rights violations. Now a prominent member of the UN Adolescent Youth Panel in Moldova, she also serves as an ambassador for the 'Block the Hatred, Share the Love' EU programme. Anghelina believes that children play a crucial role in shaping their future and has pioneered child-friendly processes and actively involved more young people in political and human rights decision-making processes.

'The rights of children are in crisis all over the world. In Palestine, Israel, Ukraine, children are suffering the most. We cannot just send out messages on social media, we need to do real actions and involve children that have gone through the same experiences,' Anghelina said.

Fran is a 15-year-old from Opatija, Croatia. With its Children's City Council that was instituted 21 years ago, he calls Opatija a 'child-friendly city,' where young people's views are considered. In addition to his work with the Children's Advisory Team, he is part of the National Eurochild Forum of Croatia and the Mediterranean Children's Movement. His main focus is promoting children's rights, including their right to participation at the local, national, and international levels.

'The world has changed a lot these past few years. It is becoming a new place for all of us. Some adults might have forgotten how it was to be a child, but if they listen to them, they will remember those beautiful places in childhood,' Fran said. 'It is important for children to be present at this event because we can voice our opinions on what we think about the world today and what we want to make of it.'

Throughout 2023, the Child Advisors have worked with Child Rights Connect and UN Human Rights to develop child-friendly materials to promote the Human Rights 75 Initiative and build the capacity of children worldwide to engage in the initiative. The resources developed by the Child Advisors and Child Rights Connect include an information sheet on UN Human Rights and a child-friendly version of the Universal Declaration of Human Rights.

'This project with Child Rights Connect and their Child Advisors allowed us to bring the voices of children from around the world to the heart of the Human Rights 75 Initiative,' said Imma Guerras-Delgado, UN Human Rights' Coordinator of the Child and Youth Rights Unit. 'We were able to hear directly from children about what is needed to make a fairer future for all with human rights at the centre.'

The Child Advisors, Child Rights Connect, and UN Human Rights also co-designed a global children's survey whose findings were summarised in the Children's Vision for Human Rights report that they presented during the Human Rights 75 high-level event. In the report, the Child Advisors ask the UN Human Rights Office to increase its collaboration with children as equal stakeholders and contributors at international, national, and local levels; expand the UN's geographic outreach to ensure equitable participation of all children in the UN's work; provide children with human rights training, information, and financial and technical support online and offline in accessible languages and formats; and strengthen human rights knowledge and awareness for children and adults at the community level.

'The Human Rights 75 Initiative and the collaboration between UN Human Rights and our Children's Advisory Team has been a great example of meaningful child participation and of child rights mainstreaming within the UN system. Our child advisers were able to work on various aspects of the initiative, from creating child-friendly documents to participating in focus group discussions with UN Human Rights by assisting with the interpretation of the data collected from children for the 'Children's Vision for Human Rights report,' said Alex Conte, Executive Director of Child Rights Connect.

'We warmly welcome the efforts of UN Human Rights in ensuring that children are integrated in their work and for giving them participation opportunities throughout the Human Rights 75 initiative.'

19 February 2024

Think!

If you could be a young activist for human rights, what would you campaign for?

What could you contribute to make a fairer future for all?

⇒ From www.ohchr.org/en/stories/2024/02/young-activists-share-their-vision-human-rights, by The Office of the High Commissioner for Human Rights, ©2024 United Nations. Reprinted with the permission of the United Nations.

The above information is reprinted with kind permission from The Office of the High Commissioner for Human Rights.

© OHCHR 1996-2024

www.ohchr.org

Useful Websites

Useful websites

www.amnesty.org.uk

www.antislavery.org

www.democracyparadox.com

www.eachother.org.uk

www.freedomfromtorture.org

www.friendsoftheearth.uk

www.hrf.org

www.independent.co.uk

www.libertyhumanrights.org.uk

www.ohchr.org

www.rescue.org

www.secularism.org.uk

www.theguardian.com

www.walkfree.org

www.weforum.org

Absolute poverty

Inability to meet even the most basic survival needs. This includes the necessities such as food, water, shelter, clothing, and healthcare.

Activism

Campaigning to bring about political or social change.

Boycott

A form of activism in which consumers refuse to buy a product or use a service to protest against unethical practices by the manufacturer/provider.

Censorship

When there are restrictions on what people can see or hear and on the information they are allowed to access, this is called censorship. By censoring something, an individual, publication, or government is preventing the whole truth from coming out or stopping something from being heard or seen at all. Items may also be censored or restricted to protect vulnerable people such as children, and to prevent public offence.

Child exploitation

Child exploitation is a broad term which includes forced or dangerous labour, child trafficking and child prostitution. The term is used to refer to situations where children are abused – physically, verbally or sexually – or when they are submitted to unsatisfactory conditions as part of their forced or voluntary employment.

Child labour

There is no universally accepted definition of child labour. However, it might generally be said to be work for children that harms or exploits them in some way (physically, mentally, morally, or by blocking access to education). According to the International Labour Organization, more than 168 million children worldwide are still in child labour and 85 million at least are subject to its worst forms (are in hazardous work).

Child marriage

Where children, often before they have reached puberty, are given to be married – often to a person many years older.

Children's rights

The Convention on the Rights of the Child (CRC) is a human rights treaty which has changed the way that children are viewed and treated since it was established in 1989. The treat sets out the civil, political, economic, social, health and cultural rights of children.

Discrimination

Unfair treatment of someone because of the group/class they belong to.

Domestic servitude

A type of labour trafficking. Domestic workers perform household tasks such as child-care, cleaning, laundry, and cooking.

Equality

The right of different groups of people to have a similar position, and/or receive the same treatment.

Glossary

Equality Act 2010

This act brings a number of existing laws together in one place. It sets out the personal characteristics that are protected by law, and behaviour which is unlawful. The 'protected characteristics' are age; disability; gender reassignment; marriage and civil partnership; pregnancy and maternity; race; religion and belief; sex and sexual orientation. Under the a,ct people are not allowed to discriminate against, harass or victimise another person because they have any of the protected characteristics.

European Convention on Human Rights

The European Convention on Human Rights was adopted by the Council of Europe in 1950 to enshrine the articles of the Universal Declaration of Human Rights, a declaration drafted in the aftermath of the Second World War in response to the atrocities of the Holocaust. The UK signed up to the Convention in 1951.

Forced labour

When someone is forced to work, or provide services, against their will. This is often the result of a person being trafficked into another country and then having their passport withheld, or threats made against their family.

Forced marriage

A marriage that takes place without the consent of one or both parties. Forced marriage is not the same as arranged marriage, which is organised by family or friends but which both parties freely enter into.

Hate crime

Hate crime is criminal behaviour where the perpetrator is motivated by hostility or demonstrates hostility towards the victim's disability, race, religion, sexual orientation, or transgender identity. These things are 'protected characteristics'. A hate crime can include verbal abuse, intimidation, threats, harassment, assault, and bullying, as well as damage to property.

Human rights

The basic rights all human beings are entitled to, regardless of who they are, where they live, or what they do. Concepts of human rights have been present throughout history, but our modern understanding of the term emerged as a response to the horrific events of the Holocaust. While some human rights, such as the right not to be tortured, are absolute, others can be limited in certain circumstances: for example, someone can have their right to free expression limited if it is found they are guilty of inciting racial hatred.

Human trafficking

The transport and/or trade of people from one area to another, usually for the purpose of forcing them into labour or prostitution.

Humanitarian intervention

When a state uses military force against another state whose military action is violating citizens' human rights.

International Human Rights Law

A set of global legal rules designed to protect the rights and freedoms of individuals and groups, and to ensure that states follow, respect, and fulfil these obligations.

Millennium Development Goals (MDG)

Agreed upon by 193 United Nations member states, the Millennium Development Goals are the world's targets for addressing poverty, education, disease, equality and environmental sustainability (made up of eight goals). For example, one goal is to eradicate extreme poverty and hunger. The aim was to achieve these goals by the year 2015. The MDGs are now replaced by the Sustainable Development Goals (SDGs).

Slavery

A slave is someone who is denied their freedom, forced to work without pay, and considered to be literally someone else's property. Although slavery is officially banned internationally, there are an estimated 27 million slaves worldwide. Article 4 of the Universal Declaration of Human Rights states that 'No one shall be held in slavery or servitude; slavery and the slave trade shall be prohibited in all their forms'.

The Human Rights Act

The Human Rights Act is a written law (statute) passed in 1998 which is in force in England and Wales. The rights that are protected by this law are based on the articles of the European Convention on Human Rights. There is an ongoing debate between supporters of the Act and its critics as to whether it should be kept, or replaced with a new UK Bill of Rights.

Torture

Intentionally causing a person physical or mental pain or suffering in order to obtain information or force them to make a confession. Under Article 5 of the Universal Declaration of Human Rights, 'No one shall be subjected to torture or to cruel, inhuman, or degrading treatment or punishment'. The subject of torture, and whether it might be considered a necessary evil in the war against terror, has recently been the subject of controversy.

United Nations Convention on the Rights of the Child (UNCRC)

An international human rights treaty that protects the rights of all children and young people under 18. The UK signed the convention on 19 April 1990 and ratified it on 16 December 1991. When a country ratifies the convention it agrees to do everything it can to implement it. Every country in the world has signed the convention except the USA and Somalia.

Universal Declaration of Human Rights

The first international, secular agreement on what were formerly called 'the rights of man,' which arose from the desire of the world's governments to prevent the recurrence of the atrocities of the Second World War by setting out a shared bill of rights for all peoples and all nations. The text is non-binding, but it retains its force as the primary authority on human rights, and has been supported by the UN's ongoing work to encourage its incorporation into domestic laws.

Index

A
absolute rights 5
activists 37–39, 40–41
asylum seekers 6, 11, 32, 33

B
balancing rights and restrictions 4
Brexit 6, 33

C
Cassin, René 10
children 31, 32, 40–41
China 16
crime, modern slavery and 30, 32

D
democracies 4

E
European Convention on Human Rights
   (ECHR) 4, 5–6, 10–11, 12–13

F
FIFA 19, 22–25
forced labour 26–27, 28–29, 30, 31
forced marriage 31
freedom of speech 17, 34

G
Gaza 16
global application of human rights 16

H
Holocaust 7, 10–11, 14, 15
Human Rights 75 40–41
Human Rights Act (UK) 1988 4–5, 13

I
Illegal Immigration Bill 33
Islamic states 17–18

L
Lauterpacht, Hersch 10–11, 14
limited rights 5

M
migrant workers
   modern slavery 29, 30, 31–33
   Qatar 19–20, 21–23

N
nature, rights of 15
Northern Ireland 13

O
organ trafficking 31

Q
Qatar 19–20, 21–23

qualified rights 4–5

R
refugees 11, 32
religion 17–18

S
Saudi Arabia 34–36
selective application 16
sexual exploitation 30–31
slavery, modern
   statistics 26, 28–29, 30
   those at risk 31–32
   types 26–27
   in the UK 30–33
Sport & Rights Alliance 24–25

T
threats to rights 6, 11, 33
torture 6, 34
types of rights 4–5

U
United Kingdom
   ECHR 10–11, 12–13
   Human Rights Act 4–6
   modern slavery 30–33
Universal Declaration of Human Rights
   7–9, 10, 14–15
universality of rights 16, 17–18

W
western values 17–18
women 34, 35–36, 37–39
World Cups 19–20, 21–23, 24–25